MAKING SENSE OF
BUSINESS REFERENCE

MAKING SENSE OF BUSINESS REFERENCE

A Guide for Librarians and Research Professionals

CELIA ROSS

AMERICAN LIBRARY ASSOCIATION

Chicago   2013

CELIA ROSS has worked in business reference in a variety of settings, from a small venture capital firm to a global consulting firm and in public and academic libraries. Along the way, she learned many of the skills and techniques she describes in this book. She is past chair of the Business Reference and Services Section (BRASS) of ALA's Reference and User Services Association (RUSA) and teaches an online course through RUSA on business librarianship. She has presented at conferences and written journal articles and book chapters on business reference. Currently she is a librarian at the University of Michigan's Kresge Business Administration Library.

ISBN: 978-0-8389-1084-9 (paper); 978-0-8389-9595-2 (PDF); 978-0-8389-9596-9 (ePub); 978-0-8389-9597-6 (Kindle). For more information on digital formats, visit the ALA Store at alastore.ala.org and select eEditions.

Library of Congress Cataloging-in-Publication Data
Ross, Celia.
    Making sense of business reference : a guide for librarians and research
professionals / Celia Ross.
      pages   cm
      Includes bibliographical references and index.
      ISBN 978-0-8389-1084-9 (alk. paper)
      1. Business libraries—Reference services. 2. Business—Bibliography—Methodology. 3. Business
literature—Bibliography—Methodology. I. Title.
      Z711.6.B87R67 2013
      025.5'27665—dc23   2012003524

Cover design by Casey Bayer. Cover image ©VolsKinvols/Shutterstock.
Text design by Karen Sheets de Gracia in Quicksand and Charis SIL.

♾ This paper meets the requirements of ANSI/NISO Z39.48-1992 (Permanence of Paper).

Printed in the United States of America

17 16 15 14 13   5 4 3 2 1

For Jack, for everything,
especially for Josie and Harriet Jane

and

For my mom,
for taking me to the library again and again

CONTENTS

PREFACE

N O ONE IS safe from business reference. If you're a reference librarian or researcher, business questions can pop up unexpectedly and then tenaciously take hold like an invasive plant species in your well-tended general subject knowledge garden. You may be noticing this happening to you more and more as recent economic conditions have driven waves of people to public and academic libraries looking for advice and resources related to business topics. Libraries of all kinds, including corporate and other special libraries, face increasing demands to provide more business information, faster, and with fewer resources than in the past. On top of all this, many emerging academic and scientific disciplines have become amalgams of liberal arts, humanities, medical, and engineering topics, all with a solid underpinning of business to boot. And even if you work in a setting where business research is not out of the ordinary, you may have noticed that the questions you're facing are getting harder and harder—students and other researchers may spend countless hours online or in databases looking for business information before turning to you for assistance. And where are we, as trained professionals, supposed to find this information? Is it hidden in that expensive, proprietary business database? Is it hiding in plain sight on the Internet, just waiting for the right combination of keywords and search strategies to unveil itself? Business information is everywhere and nowhere, it would seem. It's no wonder that a business reference question can throw even the most unflappable librarian into a bit of a tizzy. *Making Sense of Business Reference* to the rescue!

A LITTLE BIT ABOUT THIS BOOK

If bookstores or libraries had a business reference self-help section, this book would be in it. This book is your business reference friend. Depending on your background, this book will serve as a business reference primer, business reference therapy guide, a business reference refresher course, or some combination of all three. Welcome to *Making Sense of Business Reference*, one and all! Looking to learn more about the topic of business reference? Then this book is for you! Hoping to overcome your mild-to-severe business reference phobia? You've also come to the right place! Want to brush up on your business reference skills and possibly learn a new trick or two? Then dig in and start turning the pages!

In this book I share my perspective on how to evaluate a wide range of business reference questions as well as give you a sense of what information is available and the resources, both free and fee-based, that provide it. I will try to place the business reference process itself in context so that you will come away with a better understanding of which resources to turn to (and why), as well as an improved level of confidence in your business research abilities.

This book is arranged so that the business reference process is presented first, followed by an overview of the types of resources you can expect to use when dealing with business reference questions, including some of the major business databases. Then the book dives into some of the narrower topics of business reference, like industry research or investing, and highlights some of the resources to be aware of in those specific areas. Resources will generally be listed in descending order of importance or relevance, at least from my perspective—your mileage may vary, and you may favor certain resources over others and rank them differently. Finally, some miscellaneous tips and resources that didn't fit handily into any of other categories are covered before a last review of everything. A final section contains "real life" business reference stumper questions (and strategies for answering them).

Ideally, you'll read through the next chapters covering the business reference interview, the business reference question and the business reference resource first and then either continue reading through the chapters sequentially (until you get to the shocking twist ending . . . spoiler alert: even *you* can do business reference!) or dip in at will to the topics that interest—or terrify—you the most. And, if you find yourself on the spot at the desk having a brain freeze, you can even use this book as a handy cheat sheet by distracting your patron ("Look! Is that Warren Buffet handing out money and financial advice over there by the circulation desk?!") and then frantically turning to the section on, say, company research or small business to find some inspiration or clues. Also, most of the topics chapters include a special "Start Making Sense!" feature that provides you with some easy and instantly implementable exercises for applying your newfound business reference knowledge. You might also want to skim the Stumpers section initially and then revisit it as you go through some of the chapters of the book. Hopefully those stumpers won't seem so challenging once you've started to make sense of business reference.

That all said, this book is not a comprehensive guide to business and industry reference sources—many of those exist already and can be highly useful in the right situation. In fact, examples of such works are noted in the collection development section of chapter 11. This book is also not a work that assumes you have much familiarity with business terminology, acronyms or definitions—beginners are welcome. It *is* assumed that you know your way around basic general reference resources and research strategies. Finally, it's important to realize that this book is not going to make you a business reference expert in and of itself. Sorry, but merely reading a book on business reference, even a really good book on business reference (I'll let you be the judge of this book), is not enough for anyone to truly make sense of the business reference process. Like any skill, only through practice and time can you expect to become totally comfortable and confident in your abilities.

Rest assured that this book will enhance your business reference foundation, giving you the confidence to take on future business reference questions without trepidation. Ultimately, this book will show you that you already possess the skills and wherewithal as a trained librarian or researcher to effectively tackle most any kind of business reference question that comes your way. The key will be to focus on the process itself that underlies business research. Understanding this process will provide a framework to build upon for librarians and other researchers alike as you encounter business reference questions in the future.

A LITTLE BIT ABOUT THE AUTHOR

I consider myself an accidental business librarian. I am compelled to write this book because it is something I wish had been available back when I first stumbled into business reference. Business research, more than many other subject areas, carries with it an aura of fear and intimidation that I haven't seen paralleled even by tough reference questions from other disciplines. It is this formidable and sometimes unnerving association people often make with business research that I hope to alleviate with this book. If nothing else, I hope that after reading this book your urge to dive under the reference desk in fear whenever faced with a business question will be somewhat abated.

I have an undergraduate background in the humanities and science; I went to library school mostly because I didn't want to have to pick just one subject area to focus on in graduate school. I never planned on becoming a business librarian. I never took a business reference course in library school—the thought never occurred to me, and I'm not sure any were even offered. Through no conscious choice on my part, the jobs I've held during and since library school have all involved some angle of business reference, and so, in fits and starts, I eventually built up my business research background. How I ever ended up a business reference librarian still seems surreal to me, even now as I write a book called *Making Sense of Business Reference*.

HERE'S HOW IT ALL HAPPENED

A friend from library school had been hired as a librarian for a small venture capital firm and needed an assistant, and I needed an internship while I was finishing my master of science in information. With a logic that should give hope to any aspiring business researcher with little or no business experience, the founder of this venture capital firm had wanted to hire new MSI/MLS graduates of the University of Michigan's School of Information rather than MBAs from the business school, thinking that it would be easier to teach the business side of the process to a librarian than to teach the research side to a business graduate. This was lucky for me, since at that point I didn't even know what a venture capital firm was. During this semester-long internship I began to learn the basics of company and industry research. Then I graduated and went to work for a large regional branch of the Chicago Public Library. Here I was faced periodically with business-related questions and was thankful for the brief but solid foundation I had developed—but I still didn't believe that I would ever need, or want, to know more than the very basics of business reference. I was weighing the merits of my public library position and keeping my eye out for new opportunities when a friend of a friend at a global consulting firm mentioned that they were looking for a researcher. I dove headlong into the world of competitive intelligence when I was able to convince McKinsey & Company (which I'd never heard of at the time—turns out that they're a globally renowned management consulting firm) that I could earn my keep in a fast-paced, high-pressure, all-business-research-all-the-time environment. It is here where I really built up my business research repertoire, but not without a lot of support and guidance from my coworkers and from other professional colleagues whom I quickly learned were ready and willing to help as long as I thought to ask.

Eventually I left McKinsey and returned voluntarily to the library world—this is where I am happiest and where I feel I can use my skills to the fullest. I enjoy showing others how to find business and other information rather than being responsible for "deliverables" and billable hours and the other trappings of the corporate setting. And because I have stared down business reference questions in a number of venues, from that small venture capital firm to a public library and from a multibillion dollar consulting firm to academic settings, I wanted to share this experience with others who might feel the way I used to. I understand how it feels to face a stream of acronyms and jargon—NAICS, ROI, EBITDA, 10Ks, and balance sheets—and not know how to begin to interpret what I'm hearing.

In summary, if I can do it, then you, too, can become a business reference whiz! There's nothing to be afraid of, so turn the page and let's start making sense.

ACKNOWLEDGMENTS

I would like to acknowledge all the amazing librarians and other people I have encountered along this accidental path to business librarianship. This book is a direct result of their generous sharing of time, wisdom, humor, and various other forms of encouragement along the way. Special thanks go out to Elizabeth Stephan for not laughing at me when I asked her to be my first reader and for wielding her "mad editing skillz" on this manuscript; to Ben Bunnell, who started all of this back when he suggested I join him at Avalon Investments; to Rudy Barajas, who, whether he realizes it or not, is the best business research mentor ever and who—along with Eric Marohn, Tom Skiles, Matt Lopez, and others whom I'm sure I'm overlooking—made my time at McKinsey full of learning and fun; to Paula Dempsey, supervisor extraordinaire, and the rest of the Loop librarians and my other DePaul colleagues for fighting the good fight; to Arlie Sims and my Columbia College Chicago colleagues for showing me that I can't escape business reference, even at an arts and film school; to all my BRASS colleagues who are out there in the trenches every day helping people make sense of business reference and who helped me to find my ALA home; and to Corey Seeman, my current boss, and the rest of my fellow Kresge whale-petters for bringing me fully over to the dark side of this all-business-reference-all-the-time library world, and for the support (and doughnuts) you provided as I *finally* finished this book.

THE BUSINESS REFERENCE QUESTION

I N THIS CHAPTER WE'LL examine business reference questions and learn how to break them down into manageable pieces. Breaking down a business reference question into its core parts can help you to simplify and clarify it. Once you've identified a question's core components you'll have a better idea of how to approach it and which resources to turn to for finding answers.

But before we dive into the business reference question, let's first go back to basics.

START WITH WHAT YOU KNOW

When you're faced with a business reference question and you're not quite sure how to approach it, it's easy to panic and freeze up. Keep in mind, though, that business reference questions are merely "regular" reference questions that happen to be about business. And as a trained research professional, you know what you're doing—really! Remembering this is one of the most, if not *the* most, important keys to answering business reference questions.

Secret Business Reference Tip #1

A thorough reference interview is key to a successful business reference transaction.

Business reference questions can sometimes take you by surprise and throw you off your game. In your panic to answer, the reference interview can be rushed or even overlooked. Return to your reference roots and don't forget the basic starting point of the reference interview. Think back to your reference interview class (or look up *reference interview* and refresh your memory)—a lot of this is asking questions and thinking creatively, and you know how to do this. It's easy, though, to let your business reference fears get the better of you and to forget this in the heat of the business reference moment. Take a deep breath and clarify what the patron is looking for before you dive headlong into the vast sea of potential sources of information. In most reference situations, and perhaps especially in business reference situations, you should rarely assume that patrons are asking for what they really want. Even if they *are* asking for what they want, it's possible that you can offer them even more than they expect if you take the opportunity to hear them out and delve a little below the surface of their initial question.

Here's a quick refresher on reference interview basics:

Listen to the question and make sure you understand what the patron is looking for.

Partner with the patron and use what you both know (or don't know) to guide the research process.

Don't be afraid to ask questions for clarification. Ask some open- and closed-ended questions and paraphrase the question in your own words:

- Open example: What kinds of information are you looking for on the widget industry?
- Closed example: Are you looking for the global market size of the widget industry, or just the U.S. market?
- Paraphrase example: So you're looking for quarterly sales for Company X?

As your business reference knowledge—and confidence—build, your ability to paraphrase and to ask targeted open- and closed-ended questions will improve. One of my favorite questions, which works in many kinds of reference situations, is: "If I could give you exactly what you were searching for, what would it look like?" This puts the ball back in the patron's court and can help give you some time and perhaps a better idea of what they really need.

In addition to the questions you ask the patron as part of the reference inter-view, you want to ask yourself some questions, too, to make sure you're heading in the right direction. For example, ask yourself, "What does the patron really want to know?" In other words, what is their *real* question? Don't be misled by someone who throws around terminology or buzzwords. And don't be afraid to ask them to define these terms and buzzwords, especially if you yourself don't understand them. You may find they don't actually know what the terms mean, either—maybe they heard the terms somewhere or a professor uses them in class. Either way, once you get your patron talking in their own language you'll be that much closer to getting on the same page, from which you can then move forward.

Also, who is this patron asking the question? A business professional? A student? A faculty member? An entrepreneur? What do they need the info for? Are they fact-checking? "Getting smart"? Also, when do they need the info? Can you find *some* info to get them started and then get back to them? Or maybe send them off to check a particular source while you dig through others? Business reference hardly ever boils down to a simple question and a simple answer, so don't be afraid to take some time to get your bearings and explain to the patron the complexity of the task at hand. Chances are they've spent a good amount of time looking for the answer, too, and will hopefully not expect instant gratification.

For now, just know that you already have a strong foundation upon which to build your business reference home. Not only are you able to handle tough reference questions on any topic, when it comes to business you have additional subject expertise that you might not even realize. You've shopped (retail, grocery, apparel, footwear, consumer electronics, etc.), you've eaten (agriculture and food manufacturing, restaurants), you've flown (airlines), driven a car (automotive), gone to the doctor (health care), used a cell phone (telecommunications), used an ATM or credit card (banking), balanced a checkbook (finance and accounting), watched TV and gone to the movies (entertainment), and more! You get the picture. Granted, it's not always that simple, but it's not that scary, either.

BUSINESS REFERENCE SANITY CHECK

You'll sometimes find yourself in a business reference situation where you're digging and digging and coming up empty-handed and either blaming your library's lack of expensive business databases (where the answer *must* be hiding) or blaming yourself and your perceived lack of business reference knowledge for this failure. Stop right there, though, and take heart. Whether you're a business reference novice or expert and regardless of the business databases you may or may not have, there are times when the particular piece of information a patron is looking for is just not going to be found.

Secret Business Reference Tip #2

Some business reference questions can't be answered.

Yes, you heard that right. One thing to keep in mind when faced with any kind of business reference question is that *not every question can be answered*. This may be the most important advice this book has to offer. In fact, beware the business reference question with a seemingly obvious answer. It's often the question that seems so simple at first that will ultimately prove the most challenging. Of course, as a novice business librarian, it can be tricky to tell exactly which questions can and can't be answered, but just knowing that there is not always an answer can be a relief in some cases.

As we delve more deeply into business reference questions and resources, the elusive nature of some of the data that people are often looking for will become more evident. This doesn't mean you can sit back and say, "Oh, that's probably one of those questions that just can't be answered." Instead, it's more of a flag that you'll have to be that much more creative and tenacious in your searching. Just know that with many business reference questions you'll often have to rethink the initial approach and work with the patron to come up with an acceptable alternative. As with many reference scenarios, the alternative you come up with might be just as good, if not better, than what the patron originally thought they wanted.

Use your instincts and ask yourself some questions:

Would a company want its competitors to know this?
Is this kind of data even tracked? If so, would a company release it?
    For free?
Is there an alternate way to approach this question?

So, what can you do when faced with the seemingly impossible question that can't be answered? Here are some tips to keep in mind throughout the business reference interview and especially later as you dive into trying to answer the question:

Regardless of where you look for information, constantly be on the lookout for clues. Follow leads and don't get hung up on trying to find the *exact* answer.

Look for sources, not just data. This is especially true for online searching: remember that a lot is buried in the hidden Web, which means it might not come to the surface with even the most advanced googling. Try to track back to the original source of data and then drill down. Ask yourself, "Who cares about this kind of information?" to help identify these potential sources.

Think creatively! Remember to consider synonyms and employ search tricks (like wildcards, truncation, and proximity searching) and other strategies and keep an open mind when it comes to where you might find answers.

Break out whatever question you're dealing with into manageable chunks and chip away at them rather than take on a complex question all at once. Many business reference questions are fairly involved, and it often takes time to build an answer. A useful analogy I once heard someone use compared the business research process as a hunt for pieces of the puzzle, not a search for the holy grail.

Speaking of time—take a deep breath and forget about the clock: all this digging and creative thinking will take time. Don't be afraid to ask for some time to dig and get back to the person. Remove some of that "ticking time bomb" pressure—most business reference questions can't be answered with just a quick search. At the very least, you might be able to buy yourself some time by distracting the patron with a source to look through while you search in another.

Know when to say when if your wheels are spinning or you've hit a wall. Don't be afraid to step back and rethink your strategy or, even better, ask for help.

These tips will resurface throughout the rest of this book. Hopefully each chapter will give you some good ideas for where to look for clues as well as various strategies for how to approach various types of business reference questions.

One thing you can do as you familiarize yourself with the sources covered in this book is to pick a favorite company or industry and see what you can find in the different databases and other resources. Can't think of any companies? Try Apple and Microsoft or Target and Walmart or your favorite grocery store or bank. Can't think of an industry? Figure out how to browse through the content of some of the sources and see if anything jumps out, or try an industry mentioned earlier. Or scan the business news online or in the paper and use it to get inspired (okay, maybe inspired isn't the right word!). And try out the "Start Making Sense!" exercises at the end of most of the chapters.

Don't forget: You're a trained research professional, gosh darn it! An info-wrangler, a reference maverick, a research maven. The reference and research skills that got you to where you are today are subject agnostic. Also, like any skill, the more you do this, the better you will get. So, seasoned pros, take heart—you've got reference money in the bank here! And research newbies, don't worry—all the time you spend at a reference desk is an investment in your info future, whether it will hold business reference questions galore or other topics.

THE CORE FOUR

The essence of many business reference questions can be broken into four general categories, or what I like to call the *Core Four*, of information.

Patrons who are asking a business reference question are generally looking for something that falls under one or more of the following categories:

■ Company information
■ Industry information

- Investing/financial information
- Consumer information/business statistics

This is admittedly a very simplified approach. Of course, there are other areas of business reference that stretch the limits of these categories, like questions involving regulatory or legal issues, for example, or those with a focus on international data or small business financing. And, yes, some of the categories are kind of bulked together, as with investing and financial or the consumer/statistics categories. However, starting with these basics can often help you determine the best strategies for solving even the most stumpifying of business reference stumpers. Also, *Core Four* sounds better than *Core Six*, doesn't it?

This section of the book looks at some examples of the kinds of questions you might run across that can be considered business reference. Remember that the subject area of business can go way beyond standard company and industry questions and can touch upon lots of other subject areas, such as marketing or advertising, economics and government, management, or accounting. Some of these sample questions may seem more straightforward than others. Some may look like Greek to you (or another language, if you in fact speak Greek). Don't worry about that for now. Just understand that business reference questions can come in many shapes and sizes and degrees of complexity.

Figure 1.1 provides some example questions and illustrates what likely sounds like a cacophony of random business questions being shouted at you from multiple directions at the reference desk. However, looking at these examples of business

Can you point me toward where to find information on the smoothie industry?

Who are the top executives at EDS?

What is the market share of American Airlines?

What is the target market for iPods?

What are the quarterly sales and EBITDA for each Starbucks location in Michigan?

What was AOL's stock price on 4/25/05? What were their 2001 sales?

What is the most current national unemployment rate?

Where is your RMA guide?

FIGURE 1.1

reference questions through the lens of the Core Four, you can lower the volume, so to speak, and break down each question to its basic elements, even if you don't have much business reference expertise. If you find yourself struggling with any of them—and there are one or two trick questions in the example list—then that's a signal to kick up the business reference interview a notch.

Here is the list of example business reference questions from figure 1.1 again, with their accompanying Core Four category or categories.

Who are the top executives at EDS? *Company information*

What is the most current national unemployment rate? *Statistical/demographic information*

What was AOL's stock price on 4/25/05? What were their 2001 sales? *Combo: company and stock/financial information*

What is the market share of American Airlines? *Combo: industry and company information*

What are the quarterly sales and EBITDA for each Starbucks location in Michigan? *Combo: company and financial information*

Where is your RMA guide? *Depends: company financials or industry information, or both (a trick question if you're unfamiliar with this source—we'll cover it in chapter 5, "Company Finance," in the section "Industry and Financial Ratios")*

Can you point me toward where to find information on the smoothie industry? *Industry information*

What is the target market for iPods? *Combo: statistical/demographic and industry information*

Later in this book, we'll dive into each of the Core Four categories and then some, so don't worry if the categories for each of the questions isn't immediately obvious to you. For now, consider this the warm-up portion of your business reference workout and get ready to pump some business reference iron in the later chapters!

A QUICK NOTE ABOUT TEACHABLE MOMENTS

When you're in the throes of the business reference interview and throughout the time you spend working on answering the question at hand, try to grab on to those teachable moments and strive to exceed expectations, both the patron's and your own. You will be doing both yourself and the patron a service if you think aloud as you work with them to answer their questions. Describe what you are doing and what resources you are using and articulate your steps and thoughts. You'll become more adept at this kind of thinking aloud as you gain more experience in this area, but keeping the patron engaged and part of the process will benefit both of you in the long run. There will be many times when a business reference question isn't just a quick "check this resource, here's your answer" kind of situation. Use the business reference interview to educate the patron, and to remind yourself, that business research is a process. I like to tell patrons that it's called research for a reason—first you search, then you re-search, and then you search again. There's also a reason that they couldn't just google the question and find what they're looking for, and as you partner with them to tackle their question head on, you can help them realize that business research takes patience, creative thinking, and tenacity. It's also important to remember that it's not necessarily the case that you yourself will be doing all the digging and research, but rather you'll show the patron where to go and give them some search tips to try out on their own, so that they can grow their own research and database-searching skills.

As you'll discover throughout this book, business reference is not the most straightforward of processes, and this thinking aloud will not only serve as instruction for the patron, but also open opportunities for them to clarify or to notice something additional they can use. And when you're thinking aloud you offer the chance for a colleague to overhear and perhaps jump in with a suggestion—when it comes to tricky business reference questions, the more, the merrier!

START MAKING SENSE!

- ■ Ask your colleagues to share some business reference question examples and try to categorize them using the Core Four method.
- ■ Think about the kinds of business reference questions you deal with most often. Which of the Core Four categories come up most frequently?
- ■ Next time you have an opportunity to do so, whether with a business reference question or a "regular" one, consciously conduct a reference interview and also look for teachable moments.

2

THE BUSINESS REFERENCE RESOURCE

(AKA THE BUSINESS REFERENCE DATABASE)

N OW THAT WE know the gist of what most business reference questions are asking for, let's take a look at where we might find the answers. I try to highlight both free and fee-based resources throughout this book, as well as those available in print, but let's face it: proprietary online business databases are the bread and butter of truly efficient and successful business research. Becoming familiar with some of the many database names out there and the content that can be found in each will be an important part of making sense of business reference. Often databases are the only repositories of the information a business researcher is seeking. Which database you turn to will depend, in part at least, on what kind of information you need. Just as in general reference you learn to rely upon certain types of sources (e.g., an encyclopedia or an index rather than a monograph or a video) for different information needs, the same is true and then some when it comes to business reference databases.

CONTENT IS KEY

Your hunt for clues to questions related to the Core Four categories and beyond will take you to databases and other resources containing:

- News/trade/academic articles
- Company and/or industry profiles
- Analyst reports
- Consumer and marketing information
- International information
- Directory information
- Raw (mostly financial/economic) data

Content can overlap among databases, but some will include unique material or have particular areas of strength. For example, if you're looking for an industry profile, you'll learn that some databases have these while others won't. Similarly, some databases are better if you decide you need to do some article searching, some are better for consumer data, some better for analyst reports, some better for raw data, and so on. Most of the time you'll need to search more than one to avoid missing anything as well as to compare and contrast what you do find. Often, you'll come up empty-handed and just have to move on to the next database—this is all part of the process.

Database searching styles and preferences will vary—some of you will prefer to methodically exhaust potential resources one by one until you hit some kind of sweet spot. Others of you will take more of a "speed dating" approach and dip briefly into multiple databases in the hopes of getting that special vibe that makes you feel like one particular database might be worth spending some more time with. There's no one right way to search business databases, but as I mentioned earlier, it will ultimately be to your benefit if you can approach the business reference process overall, including searching databases, with a combination of stubbornness, patience, and creativity.

Remember, great business librarians have great information-searching skills, especially when it comes to mining for clues in complex databases like the ones described in this chapter. These skills are not innate, nor are they permanent. To stay sharp, skills need to be used regularly and updated over time. So don't just read about these databases—get out there and search early and search often. Keep up with your favorite databases by signing up for e-mail alerts or taking advantage of online training opportunities. Read up on product reviews in the library literature. Vendors often make trainers available to individuals or groups for tailored instruction. Some of the databases are complex enough that they will require some additional training or practice, but take heart knowing that many of the skills you'll develop with one database will apply to other databases, so most of the time spent searching (and re-searching) will at least be productive in that sense.

Speaking of training, there are a number of useful tutorials and guides that have been developed for various business databases either by the vendor or, more frequently, by other librarians like you who have struggled with a product in the past and have taken mercy on the rest of us. The Business Reference and Services Section (BRASS) of the American Library Association (ALA) has assembled a guide to these guides. You can find the Index to Business Database Tutorials here: http://connect.ala.org/node/75664/.

A professor I used to work with once said, "Every database has its own soul." This is definitely the case with business databases. On the surface, they may seem very similar, but as you become more familiar with the resources and with business reference in general, you'll learn which databases to turn to for a particular type of content or format. You'll also find that you develop preferences for certain databases over others, whether due to the unique content in one or the quirky interface of another. You may ultimately find yourself in the midst of a love/hate relationship with some. Whatever you do, don't get too attached to any particular database. Be prepared for changes like new interfaces, deletions or additions of content, ownership turnover, and even name changes. I can only hope that in between the writing and the publishing of this book, most of what is covered in this chapter will stay relatively stable. Because of this high probability of change, I haven't gone into exhaustive detail in describing the databases, either. Frankly, reading about a database isn't going to do much for your business reference skill set in the long run—as was mentioned in the previous paragraph, you've got to get out there and dive in and use these suckers to get to know them.

The following list of databases is arranged by content type and reflects what I feel is most noteworthy in each category. Many of the databases could be—and some are—listed under multiple categories because they contain multiple types of content (e.g., articles, industry profiles, company data). The lists are in alphabetical order within each category because for the most part there is no particular database that is better than the others, per se. I've tried to include as many of the big-name products that you'll hear referred to when the topic of business reference databases comes up, but this list is by no means exhaustive, nor do I personally promote or endorse any particular product over another.

Remember, too, that many online business databases offer separate corporate and academic versions. In most cases, the descriptions of the products below refer to the academic version; content may vary depending on the overall subscription package.

Of course, a major factor in deciding which database to turn to will involve whether or not your library or institution subscribes to it! Due to the relatively high price tags of business databases, it is unlikely that you would have access to everything listed here, although most academic business libraries and larger public libraries subscribe to at least a few of the following titles. And while these business databases are all robust in their own way, there is no single resource that covers all business-related topics comprehensively. Sorry.

ARTICLES

Articles are a familiar source of information to librarians, but they are often overlooked in the hunt for business information when people (mistakenly) believe that the answer they're looking for must be held only within a specialized company or industry database. When you're faced with a business reference question, articles can provide handy bits and pieces of information about a company, an industry, a person, or a product, among other things. Articles are often one of the few resources for information on private companies or on industries made up of small, private companies. Local newspapers can be a great source of this kind of information. And don't forget trade journals, many of which focus on highly specific industry areas. There's a trade journal out there for practically everything, from *Nation's Restaurant News* to *Floor Covering Weekly* to *Appliance Retailing* to *Ontario Sheep News* (check *Ulrich's Periodical Directory* if you don't believe me). Digging through articles is—or at least it should be—a common task when doing business research and this strategy will be referred to later in the book in many of the chapters. The following are some databases that specialize in articles related to business-related topics, but even a general news database will contain business information.

Where to Turn for Articles

- ABI/Inform
- Business and Industry
- Business Insights: Global
- Business Source Complete
- Dialog
- Factiva
- General Business File ASAP
- LexisNexis Academic
- RDS TableBase

ABI/Inform

For anyone seeking scholarly journals and trade publications on any number of business-related topics, ABI/INFORM is an excellent starting point. Produced now by ProQuest, ABI/INFORM is invaluable for business research. ProQuest offers an ABI/INFORM Complete product made up of several parts available separately: the ABI/INFORM Dateline database, which focuses on regional business news sources; the ABI/INFORM Global database, which includes company and industry information and provides indexing and full-text access to over 1,800 academic business and professional trade publications; and the ABI/INFORM Trade and Industry database, which includes newsletters and other publications covering a wide variety of industries. ABI/INFORM can also be searched via Dialog (see below).

Business and Industry

Business and Industry (B&I) database from Gale Cengage Learning provides access to thousands of trade journals and other reports. This in and of itself is great, but what makes B&I notable is its unique search features. Rather than the traditional title, author, subject, keyword options that most databases provide, B&I offers a deeper level of indexing. The search interface includes drop-down options for what they call *concept terms* (market share, market size, ad budget, target markets, etc.) and *market terms* (telemarketing, loyalty, campaign slogan, etc.) as well as the ability to limit by document type (company overview, editorial, industry overview, etc.). You can also limit by geographic area or by industry. Here's a link to an interesting set of B&I search examples: www.gale.com/customer_service/ sample_searches/bi.htm. Business and Industry can also be searched via Dialog (see below).

Business Insights: Global

Business Insights: Global (BI:G) is a new product from Gale Cengage Learning. BI:G offers enhanced searching functionality and charting capabilities and provides access to thousands of scholarly trade and industry publications; case studies; global economic and statistical data from WorldBank and other sources; country profiles from Dun & Bradstreet and the Economist Intelligence Unit; and newly globalized Gale industry essays. Video content from SkillSoft's 50 Lessons (www.50lessons.com) is in the works, as are additional scholarly journals and case study collections. With an intuitive interface, BI:G allows users to quickly and easily compare companies or countries, search for articles or case studies, and more.

Business Source Complete

Although primarily known as a business journal database providing full-text journals in all disciplines of business, including marketing, management, accounting, finance, and economics, EBSCO's Business Source Complete contains full-text, nonjournal content, including thousands of company and industry profiles (from Datamonitor), country economic reports (from Economist Intelligence Unit [EIU] and Global Insight), financial data, and more. EBSCO's Business Source Complete builds upon their Business Source Elite and Premier products and also offers investment reports, conference proceedings, and expanded historical journal coverage. Business Source Complete (or any of the other iterations) is another great starting point for business reference article searching and more.

Dialog

Dialog, now owned by ProQuest, is the oldest of the old-school article databases. Predating the Internet, Dialog is actually a collection of hundreds of different databases related to business, science, law, and other topics. While Dialog isn't a database you'd offer up for general patron use, it may fit your situation if you're a solo researcher or want access to a broad range of publications on a pay-per-use basis. Originally only searchable by a fairly complicated command-based process, Dialog now offers multiple, and more user-friendly, ways of searching, although hard-core searchers will be pleased to know they can still dive in with indexed fields and codes galore. To browse through the many databases offered through Dialog, see their Bluesheets (named after the binders and binders full of blue sheets upon which the database descriptions were once printed) page here: http://library.dialog.com/bluesheets/.

Factiva

As well as being a great source of full-text journal articles from trade and industry publications, Factiva provides full-text access to local, national, and international newspapers in twenty-two languages, including the full text of the *Wall Street Journal* (Factiva's owner, Dow Jones, publishes the notable business daily. Dow Jones, in turn, is a subsidiary of the global news conglomerate News Corporation). Factiva features a company report builder that pulls together news and financial information from a number of content providers. Factiva includes global market indexes, historical stock prices, and country information. Use Factiva when you want to expand your article search beyond business publications to include global news coverage.

General Business File ASAP

General Business File ASAP indexes and provides full-text access to numerous business journals, investment reports and news wires. A subset of Gale Cengage Learning's Business and Company Resource Center, General Business File ASAP is essentially the article and news content of that product pulled out as a stand-alone database.

LexisNexis Academic

LexisNexis Academic holds a wealth of information on public and private companies. Because users can search hundreds of journals and (important for smaller company research) newspaper articles, with a bit of digging they can turn up a lot of information often not included in the primarily journal-based databases. Additionally, the business section of LexisNexis Academic includes the full text of company profiles from Hoover's, as well as Securities and Exchange Commission filings, accounting and finance journals, and more. For a supplemental fee, LexisNexis Academic subscribers can add the relatively new Company Dossier product, which has more functionality and content. LexisNexis also provides broad legal coverage, which may be useful depending on the nature of the business reference question you're dealing with.

RDS TableBase

This is an interesting combination of a full-text article database combined with raw-data indexing. TableBase takes away some of the searching for needles of data in haystacks of articles. Like Business and Industry (both are part of the RDS Business Suite from Gale Cengage Learning), indexing terms in TableBase include rankings, market share, advertising spending, and more. By taking full-text articles and indexing them to highlight the data content that can be found in them, TableBase provides the creative searcher with a lot of options for finding useful nuggets of information that require a lot more digging through more traditional article databases. TableBase content can also be searched via Dialog.

COMPANY AND INDUSTRY PROFILES

Some databases contain prepackaged reports on industries or companies. These profiles can provide handy overviews of the company or industry at hand and be full of useful clues and other information that might help in guiding the rest of your search. You may have some databases available through your library subscriptions that include this kind of packaged content. And don't forget that some business encyclopedias contain nicely synthesized overviews of companies, industries, and business leaders. The following are databases that include company and industry profiles as well as other company and industry-related data. There are specialized industry profile databases that focus on specific sectors like information technology or pharmaceuticals, but we won't go into those in this initial sweep of company and industry databases.

Where to Turn for Company and Industry Profiles

- Business and Company Resource Center (BCRC)
- Business Insights: Global
- Business Monitor Online
- Business Source Complete
- Freedonia Focus Report Collection
- Gale Directory Library
- Hoover's
- IBISWorld
- MarketLine
- MarketResearch.com Academic
- Mergent Online
- Mintel
- Morningstar
- OneSource
- Orbis
- Plunkett Research
- PrivCo
- Standard & Poor's NetAdvantage
- Statista
- Value Line Investment Survey
- Specialized industry databases

Business and Company Resource Center (BCRC)

In addition to full-text articles from industry and trade journals, Gale Cengage Learning's Business and Company Resource Center (BCRC) provides online, searchable access to a number of their print reference products, including *Ward's*

Business Directory of U.S. Private and Public Companies, Ward's Business Directory of Private and Public Companies in Canada and Mexico, Business Rankings Annual, and *Market Share Reporter.* BCRC could really fall under a number of different business reference resource categories, but because of the easy access to profiles from resources like the International Directory of Company Histories and the Encyclopedia of Emerging Industries, I tend to turn to BCRC most often for company or industry profiles. In mid- to late summer 2012, Gale Cengage Learning will transition all of the BCRC content on a new Business Insights: Essential platform. This product will be available for customers not wishing to upgrade to the full Business Insights: Global edition.

Business Insights: Global
See page 13.

Business Monitor Online
Business Monitor Online, from Business Monitor International, is an excellent source of industry data by country or region. A wide range of industry sectors is covered, including agribusiness, autos, commercial banking, consumer electronics, defense and security, food and drink, freight and transport, information technology, infrastructure, insurance, metals, mining, petrochemicals, oil and gas, pharmaceuticals, power, real estate, retail, shipping, telecommunications, textiles and clothing, tourism, and water. Business Monitor Online also covers political risk, finance, economic indicators, macroeconomic performance, and the business operating environment for a number of countries, including emerging markets and industrialized countries.

Business Source Complete
See page 13.

Freedonia Focus Report Collection
The Freedonia Focus Report Collection from the Freedonia Group primarily covers industry sectors such as energy, construction and building materials, electronics, chemicals, industrial/manufacturing, and packaging industry topics. Other sectors include consumer products, pharmaceuticals/life sciences, and service industries. This is a good database for finding coverage of somewhat niche industries, and the reports cover market size, product and market forecasts, industry composition, major players, and trends.

Gale Directory Library
For libraries that do not wish to subscribe to Gale Cengage Learning's Business Insights: Global product or the scaled-down Business Insights: Essentials version (set to replace their Business and Company Resource Center database), Gale makes some content available as individual e-directories through the Gale Directory Library. For customers who want a more traditional experience that provides

digital access while preserving the purchase model and à la carte ordering options of print, the Gale Directory Library is worth investigating.

Hoover's

Hoover's offers a lot of basic company information all in one place on thousands of public and private companies. It's a great place to start to find out whether a company is public, private, parent, or subsidiary and to get a quick snapshot of what you're dealing with. Unlike most of the databases listed in this chapter, you'll find some of Hoover's content available for free on the Hoovers.com website. However, much of the data requires a subscription. Still, I often start with a quick Hoovers.com search if I'm unfamiliar with a company and want to find out whether or not it is public, private, or a subsidiary. Hoover's content is also available through LexisNexis Academic's company profiles section.

IBISWorld

IBISWorld provides access to more than seven hundred United States and global industries, including everything from shoe stores to gold ore mining and all industries in between. An archive of older reports is available as a separate subscription, as are companion databases that cover China and other regions.

MarketLine

In addition to news and analysis, MarketLine is a great go-to source for profiles of industries as well as countries and public companies. The source of most of their packaged reports is the Datamonitor Group, so if patrons are looking specifically for Datamonitor, much of that content can be found through MarketLine.

MarketResearch.com Academic

MarketResearch.com is an aggregator of industry and other intelligence reports. MarketResearch.com Academic is the academic subscription version of that site. Full-text reports from several market research publishers can be accessed; how many publishers depends on your subscription level. Topics covered include health care, consumer goods, telecommunications, and manufacturing. Content providers include Kalorama Information (for biotechnology, diagnostics, health care, medical devices, and pharmaceuticals), Packaged Facts (food and beverage, personal care, demographics, financial services, consumer goods, retailing, etc.), SBI (house and home, manufacturing and construction, and materials and chemicals), and Simba Information (media industry).

Mergent Online

For publicly traded company profiles and financials, Mergent Online is an excellent resource. Mergent, originally Moody's, has been collecting data and rating publicly traded companies since 1900. Mergent Online covers U.S. and international companies and includes country economic reports. Company profiles include history, historical financials, and management profiles, and come with a number of exportable report-building and screening options. There is also an archive available of defunct, merged, or bankrupt companies, executive biographies, corporate calendars, and a stand-alone database containing PDF versions of historical Moody's/Mergent manuals.

Mintel

Mintel is a great resource for getting industry coverage with a heavy focus on consumers. Mintel covers food, beverage, apparel, beauty and personal, retail, travel, and more. Each study provides lots of statistics and includes primary and secondary resources. It is international in scope but strongest in European countries and the United States. Geographic coverage of the reports will vary based on your subscription level.

Morningstar

Morningstar is focused on investment research and provides stock reports on publicly traded companies as well as information on mutual funds, hedge funds, and other types of investments. Morningstar print publications are often available in public libraries. Geared primarily toward the personal investor but growing in scope to become comprehensive enough for some professional traders, Morningstar's online offerings include historical stock coverage, mutual fund ratings, and personal finance investing tools and calculators. They also produce a Securities and Exchange Commission (SEC) document-searching product called the Morningstar Document Research Center (formerly 10K Wizard).

OneSource

OneSource is another all-in-one product that features articles, directories, analyst reports, and then some, including company and industry overviews. OneSource, from InfoGroup, offers public and private company information, executive profiles, financial data, and industry intelligence, and provides powerful screening capabilities.

Orbis

Orbis's strength lies in its sweeping international coverage of public as well as private companies. This Bureau Van Dyke product allows users to search across close to 40 million companies from across the globe and includes financial and other data.

Plunkett Research

Plunkett Research publishes a number of industry almanacs that give a useful snapshot to anyone trying to get a quick overview on an industry's trends, statistics, and major players. The online version allows for all kinds of screening and reporting options. Check your stacks to see if you have any of the Plunkett almanacs in print.

PrivCo

PrivCo, a relatively new player, bills itself as the "private company financial authority." Responding to a veritable private company information desert in the company research landscape, PrivCo offers detailed information on over 42,000 private companies and also includes information on private investors, merger and acquisition activity and venture capital and private equity funding. Public companies who have been involved in private market deals (e.g., acquiring a private company) are covered to some extent. A Knowledge Bank feature provides handy overviews and explanations of the private market. PrivCo is a powerful tool for private company research and they are worth keeping an eye on as their data coverage and functionality continues to grow and improve.

Standard & Poor's NetAdvantage

For industry profiles and company profiles and analysis, Standard & Poor's (S&P) NetAdvantage is hard to beat. NetAdvantage pulls together in one online resource a number of S&P's reference publications, including stock reports, corporation records, register of public companies, and register of private companies. It also includes an online version of S&P's popular industry surveys, which are excellent resources for getting smart quickly. These surveys cover about fifty broadly defined industries and provide a glossary of industry-related terms, an industry profile, pointers to key publications and associations in the industry, a look at the industry's current environment, key industry ratios and statistics, an overview of how the industry operates, and a handy section on how to analyze that particular industry. NetAdvantage is a great source for public company financial and market information, private company directory data, and mutual fund screening. Five-year snapshots of public company financials are featured, as well as industry-related news and competitor lists. Economic and market analyses are also included. NetAdvantage has been expanding its international content by adding global industry surveys and global company reports, further enhancing this already robust product.

Statista

Statista is a relatively new product on the business reference database scene. It covers a wide variety of industries and consumer demographics, pulling data from a number of free and fee-based sources into one easy-to-search interface. Country coverage focuses on Europe and other developed countries, although data related to emerging countries can be found, too. Data sources are thoroughly cited, should users want to follow up on a lead to search for additional data, and each page points to related results for further exploration. Some free data is available, but for full content and downloading capabilities, a subscription is required. If you're hunting for specific data points related to an industry or consumers, Statista is an excellent place to start your search.

Value Line Investment Survey

For overviews and analysis of company stock performance, Value Line Investment Survey is an important tool. The online version of Value Line provides better searching and screening than the print products, which are popular with individual investors and available in many public and academic libraries. Value Line's "Ratings and Reports" section presents individual reports that give an overview of a company's stock performance and potential for future performance. Economic and market analysis is provided in Value Line's "Selection and Opinion" section; particular stocks to pay attention to are highlighted. The "Summary and Index" feature points to recent Value Line coverage and provides lists of companies ranked highly within its proprietary analysis system, which considers criteria such as timeliness and safety. Although Value Line is often only thought of as a source of investment information, there are short overviews of a number of industry sectors included in the online (and print) version of the Value Line Investment Survey.

Specialized industry databases

There are many database products available that target specific industries, such as technology, sports, medical, automotive, and more. Many of them are available for academic use, but because of the nature of this kind of specialized industry information, they are often relatively pricey and thus not often found in a public library setting. A few examples of these types of databases include Alternative Energy eTrack, Automotive News Data Center, eMarketer, Forrester, Frost and Sullivan, Gartner, Life Science Analytics, Medical eTrack, and Sports Business Research Network.

ANALYST REPORTS

Reports on companies written by financial analysts can provide useful insight into a company that may not be found in a typical overview or through an article search. There are different kinds of analysts working on Wall Street, and each kind produces a different kind of report, generally with a focus on making a recommendation to either buy or sell (or hold on to) a stock—so keep in mind that only public companies will be covered by these kinds of reports. Some reports are in-depth and are intended to catch the attention of investors; some are brief updates used by stock portfolio or pension fund managers; others are kind of in between. There is a requirement that analysts disclose the relationship they have with the company being analyzed (check the small print at the end of the report)—in most cases, companies are paying in some way for their company to be covered by a particular analyst house. This can—and should—be a red flag for you and your patrons to consider the overall objectivity and to carefully evaluate the report in hand. That said, even given this potential for bias, at the end of the day, providing in-depth company information is the goal of most analysts, so you can often find useful, detailed information in an analyst report that isn't going to be readily found in an article search or other company profiles. Also, don't forget that some data providers, such as Standard & Poor's, Business Monitor Online, and Morningstar, produce their own analyses. While not necessarily defined officially as analyst reports, since that term tends to refer to reports produced specifically by financial firms or brokerage houses, those are also excellent sources of information.

Where to Turn for Analyst Reports

- OneSource
- ThomsonONE

OneSource

Part of the company coverage provided in OneSource includes a link to analyst reports. For many of the public companies covered by OneSource, you'll find one or two recent reports from various analyst firms in addition to the company profiles they provide from the publisher GlobalData.

ThomsonONE

ThomsonONE, one of the many products available from Thomson Financial, provides access to current and historical analyst reports from a number of firms through their Thomson Research component, which also contains the analyst reports product Investext. Although it doesn't contain reports from every analyst firm out there, this is one of the most comprehensive resources for analyst reports. ThomsonONE also provides access to annual reports, SEC filings, and I/B/E/S tearsheets—analyst earnings estimates—for U.S. and international publicly traded companies, among other information.

CONSUMER INFORMATION

Finding data on consumers—their attitudes, their buying habits, their demographics, and so on—is almost always a challenge. We'll cover some of these challenges, and strategies for dealing with them, in chapter 7, "Consumer Research and Marketing/Advertising." The databases listed in this section can help you find consumer-related data, some by providing geographically based demographic data (like households with income over a certain amount in specified zip codes or which state buys the most frozen pizza) or other information that may help you and your patrons paint a more robust picture of the target market or consumer product you're researching.

Where to Turn for Consumer and Marketing Information

- Ad$pender
- Advertising Red Books
- BusinessDecision and BusinessDecision Academic
- eMarketer
- Esri Business Analyst
- Local Market Audience Analyst (from SRDS)
- Mintel
- MRI+
- Passport (formerly Global Market Information Database [GMID])
- ReferenceUSA Consumers/Lifestyle
- Simmons OneView (formerly Choices III)
- Simply Map
- Social Explorer
- Standard Rate and Data Service (SRDS) Advertising Sources
- Statista
- Wave

Ad$pender

http://kantarmediana.com/intelligence/products/adspender

Companies aren't required to report how much they spend on advertising, but Ad$pender is one of the few products out there that tracks advertising spending by brand, product category, and outlet (e.g., television, radio, billboard). Ad$pender is owned by Kantar Media, which also owns the SRDS suite of products, among other advertising and marketing resources.

Advertising Red Books

www.redbooks.com

The Advertising Red Books (sometimes referred to simply as the "Red Books") from LexisNexis track companies that spend more than $200,000 annually on advertising and provide some ad spending data, agency and brand data, and some other top-level company information. The Advertising Red Books database contains profiles of over 10,000 advertising agencies and includes a list of the accounts represented by each agency and field of specialization.

BusinessDecision and BusinessDecision Academic

For public and academic libraries, respectively, BusinessDecision and Business-Decision Academic are reporting and mapping databases that combine extensive consumer household, market segmentation, and demographic data with GIS mapping technology.

eMarketer

eMarketer was briefly mentioned earlier as an example of a specialized industry database covering online marketing and e-business, but it also provides a lot of consumer data, at least regarding consumers' online habits. Topics include Internet users by age, gender, race and other demographic breakdowns, social media, mobile phone users, and more.

Esri Business Analyst
www.esri.com/software/bao/comparison-table.html
Esri is a major name in the world of Geographic Information Systems or GIS. Their Business Analyst Online product offers detailed data about consumer spending and demographics along with powerful shopping center and business location analysis. Esri's useful print publications *Sourcebook of Zip Code Demographics* and *Sourcebook of County Demographics* ceased publication in 2009.

Local Market Audience Analyst (from SRDS)
Local Market Audience Analyst cross-tabulates demographic attributes such as age, gender, and income against those groups' likelihood to participate in a variety of activities (what they call *lifestyles*). These lifestyle activities are anything from traveling for business to exercising, hunting, owning a dog, and many others. Data is survey based and broken out by lifestyles (e.g., so you can look up who says they ride a bike to work) and by geographic area (e.g., so you can see what people in Spokane like to do) and by demographic attributes (e.g., so you can see what women ages 22–35 do compared to men ages 36–45). This database replaces the print-only *Lifestyle Market Analyst*, which ceased publication in 2008. See also the SRDS Advertising Sources products.

Mintel
See page 18.

MRI+
http://mriplus.com
The MRI+ database from GfK Mediamark Research and Intelligence provides information on demographics, lifestyles, product and brand usage, and advertising media preferences reported by a sample of more than twenty-five thousand U.S. consumers. The online version available to libraries is dated—usually at least one or two years old—but it is one of the few products that provides this kind of item/brand-level sales data while still being relatively affordable for libraries.

Passport
Passport (formerly known as Global Market Information Database, or GMID), a Euromonitor product, covers more than 200 countries and provides historical and forecast market data for consumer products as well as demographic, economic, and marketing statistics for each country. Market share data for numerous products is included, and quick top-level economic data can also be pulled to compare trends across countries and time. But the real wealth of information comes from the consumer data side of the product—find out how much people spent on pet food

or on diapers in France as compared to the whole world. Quickly export this data into handy spreadsheets.

ReferenceUSA Consumers/Lifestyle
ReferenceUSA is also mentioned below in the Directory Information section, but they are worth noting in the Consumer and Marketing section for their Consumers/Lifestyle module. Use this module to screen over 200 million U.S. consumers by various criteria such as geography, home value, and lifestyles such as charitable donors, outdoor recreation, pets and animals, politics, hobbies, and more.

Simmons OneView
Simmons OneView (formerly known as Choices III) from Experian provides survey data on the demographic, psychographic, and media use characteristics of users of products, brands, and services. Like MRI+, academic access to the surveys is generally embargoed by at least two years. Thankfully, OneView is now available to academic subscribers via an online portal instead of stand-alone discs.

Simply Map
SimplyMap allows you to create thematic maps and reports by searching across demographic, business, and marketing data culled from sources such as the U.S. Census, MRI+ (above), and Simmons OneView (above). The SimplyMap report wizard makes it easy to quickly create a ranked list of areas or to compare locations.

Social Explorer
Social Explorer, distributed by Oxford University Press, is a database that provides access to the entire U.S. Census back to 1790 as well as religious congregation member data, the U.S. Census American Community Survey, and carbon emissions data. Much of the data itself is available elsewhere freely online, but Social Explorer provides a clean, easy-to-navigate interface and additional exporting and formatting tools.

Standard Rate and Data Service (SRDS) Advertising Sources
SRDS products provide information and analysis on all kinds of media products, including consumer magazines, business publications, TV and radio stations, and newspapers. Advertising rates, circulation data, and profile information on audience markets including DMA and MSA maps are part of what you'll find in the suite of SRDS databases. When used creatively, they can provide a great deal of target market insight and other useful information. See also SRDS's Local Market Audience Analyst product.

Statista
Statista was mentioned above because of the industry data it contains, but it also provides a wealth of consumer information. From social media habits to wine consumption and more, Statista is worth a search if you're looking for anything related to consumers.

Warc

Warc, previously known as World Advertising Research Center, publishes and aggregates all kinds of material related to marketing. Content includes transcripts and reports from advertising conferences, case studies and best practice papers, as well as ad spending data.

INTERNATIONAL INFORMATION

Many resources are limited in their scope to only U.S. or North American companies and industries. The databases listed below include or even focus on international companies or provide in-depth country profiles, including industry and demographic data. I'll go over some of these resources and others that are available for free in chapter 9, "International Business." Here I highlight just a few of the fee-based databases that specifically cover international business information and are used in an academic setting. Unfortunately, many of these kinds of resources will be cost prohibitive and/or out of scope for most public libraries (although World Bank Data is available for free and highlighted in this chapter).

Where to Turn for International Information

- Business Insights: Global
- Business Monitor Online
- Economist Intelligence Unit (EIU)
- IHS Global Insight
- ISI Emerging Markets
- Passport (formerly Global Market Information Database [GMID])
- SourceOECD/OECDiLibrary
- World Bank Data

Business Insights: Global
See page 13.

Business Monitor Online
See page 16.

Economist Intelligence Unit (EIU)
For global economic data and country profiles, EIU.com is a comprehensive and robust resource. The Economist Intelligence Unit, part of the Economist Group that publishes the *Economist* magazine, covers business conditions, economic forecasting, and other data for more than two hundred countries. Additionally, some versions of EIU.com include analysis and background information for eight industry areas: automotive; food, beverages and tobacco; consumer goods and retailing; health care and pharmaceuticals; energy and electricity; telecommunications and technology; financial services; and travel and tourism.

ViewsWire, another offering from the suite of products available from the Economist Intelligence Unit, is a business intelligence product that includes coverage of the political and regulatory environment as well as economic and financial indicators for more than 195 countries, with an emphasis on those countries that are considered emerging markets.

IHS Global Insight
The IHS Global Insight database contains forecasts, country reports, sovereign and country risk ratings, and same-day analysis of the economic, political, legal, tax, operational, and security environments for a variety of industries. It also includes analysis of global legislative, regulatory, and policy developments.

ISI Emerging Markets
ISI's Emerging Market Information Service delivers news, company, and financial data on more than seventy emerging markets in Asia, Latin America, Central and Eastern Europe, the Middle East, and Africa.

Passport
See page 23.

SourceOECD/OECDiLibrary
The Organisation for Economic Co-operation and Development (OECD) produces reports and statistics on its members (currently 34, mostly high-income countries) that cover a wide variety of subjects, including economics, trade, government finance, and health. For example, the documentary film *Waiting for Superman* uses OECD education data. Previously, SourceOECD was the name of the database produced by OECD, but this will eventually—if not already by the publication of this book—be replaced by OECDiLibrary.

World Bank Data
http://data.worldbank.org
Unlike most of the other resources in this chapter, the World Bank Data site is openly and freely available. I'm including it here because it is an important source for all kinds of data related to international socioeconomic development. Some of the data, such as the World Development Indicators (WDI) and Global Development Finance (GDF), used to be available only as fee-based products.

DIRECTORY INFORMATION

If you've ever used a phone book, then you have a good idea of what a directory provides. In business reference, there are often specialized directories providing lists of companies that operate in a certain industry or in a certain state. Often directories will identify private companies in addition to public companies, albeit with limited phone book entry–type information. While there are many databases listed in this chapter that are useful for finding company information, some databases are better than others when it comes to screening (searching for companies that meet certain criteria, e.g., number of employees, industry, sales, or geography) and exporting functionality. If a patron needs to identify or generate a list of companies, these databases offer the filtering and export capabilities that will help them make the most of the data.

Where to Turn for Directory Information

- Corporate Affiliations
- D&B Million Dollar Database
- Leadership Directories
- Mergent Online
- OneSource
- Orbis
- ReferenceUSA
- Standard & Poor's NetAdvantage
- Ward's Business Directory of U.S. Private and Public Companies

Corporate Affiliations
The Corporate Affiliations database from LexisNexis is a great tool for tracking down a company's ultimate ownership. You can screen by company size, location, industry code, and even job title. Print directories, also known as "Who Owns Whom," are available as well. There are volumes for public, private, and international companies, plus a master index for company names as well as brand names.

D&B Million Dollar Database
The D&B Million Dollar Database from Dun & Bradstreet is so named because it includes information on businesses with more than $1 million in annual sales (or twenty or more employees). Data includes contact information, lists of key executives, revenues, number of employees, and other useful background information. This is another great resource to start with if you're just trying to get smart quick about a company and find out whether it's public, private, or a subsidiary.

Leadership Directories
Most often found in a public library setting, the Leadership Directories can provide a nice snapshot of a company, a nonprofit, or a financial institution (there are additional Leadership Directories published on municipal and other governmental topics) and give key contact information and other data. The print versions of some of these are often referred to as the "Yellow Books."

Mergent Online
See page 17. Mergent also allows for some filtering and exporting.

OneSource
See page 18. OneSource can also be used to screen companies by size, industry, geography, sales, and other criteria.

Orbis
See page 18. Orbis has powerful screening capabilities and a wide breadth of public and private company coverage worldwide.

ReferenceUSA
ReferenceUSA provides powerful screening and crisscross capabilities (using a number to look up an address or vice versa) for over 12 million public and private U.S. businesses.

Standard & Poor's NetAdvantage
See page 19. S&P's NetAdvantage has some screening/exporting capabilities, too.

Ward's Business Directory of U.S. Private and Public Companies (Mexico and Canada editions also available)
Available as part of Gale Cengage Learning's Business and Company Resource Center, Ward's Business Directories are also available as stand-alone products and can be used for screening companies.

RAW DATA

Often business researchers need raw data points—these can be daily stock prices, municipal bond ratings, currency exchange rates, and so on. This kind of data request can quickly turn unwieldy, whether because it requires a consistent run of data going back a number of years or because it involves complicated financial or economic data points—or some combination of these challenges. Keep in mind that every database mentioned so far contains raw data of some sort, but I am mentioning a few databases here in this section that are especially strong in churning out numbers or other data points, especially when it comes to financial and economic related information. Also note that you are unlikely to find these types of databases in public library settings or in smaller academic libraries. Because of the complexity of the data and the systems involved with these types of databases, their interfaces are generally not designed for the novice user. In other words, they are not intuitive at all and usually require some sort of training to use. Not to mention, many of them are prohibitively expensive.

Where to Turn for Raw (Mostly Financial/Economic) Data
- Bloomberg
- Center for Research in Security Prices (CRSP)
- Compustat

- Datastream
- Global Financial Data
- SDC Platinum
- ThomsonONEBanker
- Wharton Research Data Services (WRDS)
- Worldscope

Bloomberg
Bloomberg contains much more than just raw data, but for real time (and some historic) financial and market data for U.S. and global public companies, Bloomberg is considered one of the premiere resources in both professional and academic business settings.

Center for Research in Security Prices (CRSP)
CRSP (pronounced *crisp*) contains security-level historical pricing, returns, and volume data on more than 20,000 stocks (inactive and active companies) from the New York Stock Exchange (NYSE), American Stock Exchange (AMEX), and NASDAQ markets.

Compustat
From Standard & Poor's, Compustat contains fundamental financial and price data for both active and inactive publicly traded companies.

Datastream
Datastream, from Thomson Financial (part of Thomson Reuters), provides historical, global coverage of companies, stock markets, commodities, currencies, bond markets, economic data, and more. Datastream aggregates data from sources including national governments, the International Monetary Fund (IMF), and Worldscope. Harvard's Baker Library has an excellent overview for more information: www.library.hbs.edu/helpsheets/datastreamdetail.html.

Global Financial Data
Global Financial Data contains global historical data related to stock markets, currencies, commodities, and more. And in the case of Global Financial Data, *historical* means more than just going back ten to twenty years. Some of their data goes back as far as the 1200s.

SDC Platinum
SDC Platinum, now owned by Thomson Reuters, focuses on mergers and acquisitions, syndicated loans, private equity, and more.

ThomsonONE
As you may be sensing by now from the entries in this section, Thomson, as in Thomson Finance and Thomson Reuters, is a big name when it comes to finance

data. Their ThomsonONE product contains publicly traded company information and international market data, among other things. ThomsonONE contains company profiles, research reports, and other information that would normally have to be pulled together from multiple sources, including Worldscope, the SEC, First Call, and Datastream. Additional subscription content can expand coverage to include international indexes data, merger and acquisition data, historical currency data, and more.

Wharton Research Data Services (WRDS)

WRDS (pronounced *words*) provides a single Web-based interface for accessing numerous financial, accounting, banking, economics, management, marketing, and public policy databases (e.g., Compustat and CRSP).

Worldscope

Worldscope is another Thomson Reuters–owned product that contains monthly historical financial data for non-U.S. companies.

START MAKING SENSE!

- Review the online resources you have available at your institution and categorize them into company and industry, articles, raw data, and the like.
- Do some speed dating—pop into some of the databases and note your first impressions. Maybe you'll make a business database love connection!
- In tandem with the "Collection Development" section of chapter 11, review not just your collection but also your patrons and their needs and see if they align.
- Using either the Business Databases Tutorials resource mentioned in this chapter or vendor-created guides, challenge yourself to explore one or two databases that have intimidated you in the past.

3

COMPANY RESEARCH

A BUSINESS REFERENCE SCENARIO often involves looking for company information of some sort. A patron might be looking for a job and trying to identify companies in a particular industry. Even better, maybe they are preparing for an interview and wants to know as much as they can about a potential employer. They might be trying to identify competitors of a particular company, perhaps their own. They may wish to find out more about a company that makes a particular product or which companies are major players in a particular industry. In all these cases and many more, company information resources will come in handy.

Some company information questions (depending on the company, at least) involve asking for fairly basic items, such as a headquarters address or a CEO's name. But in this age of information when basic data like this is generally readily available, more often than not, the company information questions that make it to the reference desk are bumped up a notch and tend to run a little deeper, such as complex financial information requests and even internal operations questions.

As company information starts to cross into the realm of proprietary and trade secrets, it's important to keep in mind one of the secret business reference tips that was revealed earlier—namely, that not every business reference question has an answer. In other words, not all company information is openly available. This is for a reason: companies do not want their competitors to know how they do what they do, how much of it they did last year or ten years ago, or whether they do it well or not. This is not to say that with some digging and creative thinking you can't get to some deeper levels of company information. It's just something to remember when you're approached with a business reference question that involves company information.

GETTING STARTED: COMPANY RESEARCH

The first thing to determine when you're dealing with a company research question is whether the company is publicly traded, private, or a subsidiary of a larger parent company. To do this, use one of the company information databases listed in chapter 2. Knowing whether a company is public or private or parent or subsidiary will help you get a sense for where to turn for information and what you might expect to find; for example, some of the resources you'll turn to cover only public companies. You'll also want to determine whether the company is based in the United States or another country, as this may limit the types of information that are available in addition to what resources you should use. (See chapter 9, "International Business," for more information.)

A company is considered public when it has shares that are traded on a stock exchange. In the United States, public companies are regulated by the SEC and required to file information under federal securities laws. This makes it much easier, relatively speaking, to find detailed financial and other information on public companies compared to private ones, which are not subject to these same disclosure obligations. Also, many public and private companies alike are made up of smaller, subsidiary entities. Even with all the SEC regulations, public companies are not required to break out certain details about their business, including reporting on their subsidiaries separately. So, as past experience may have already taught you or as you have guessed by now, it is much harder to find information on privately held companies or subsidiaries—and harder still, on private subsidiaries. Where possible, I try to note whether a database includes coverage of private companies and/or subsidiaries. We'll discuss some additional strategies and resources to help you with these kinds of companies in chapter 5, "Company Finance."

You'll also want to consider what kind of format of the company information will best suit your patron's needs. Will a nice, packaged, fairly generic company profile do the trick? Do they need to screen companies and generate a list based on criteria like sales or geographic location? Are they looking at a particular part of a company's operations, like their marketing or supply chain? This kind of information can also be helpful as you're trying to decide which company information resource is best suited to the task at hand.

Whether you're looking for a public company, a subsidiary, or a private company, more often than not you'll want to spend part of your research time in an article database searching for information and clues. This is especially true if you're dealing with a private company or subsidiary. Don't rely on the bare-bones, phone book–like entry (if you can find even that) for the small private company you're researching. Seek out local news articles (is the company headquartered in Evanston, Illinois? Try a search of the *Chicago Tribune* or the *Chicago Sun-Times*); go to the company's website to identify CEO names and search for those, too; and identify similar companies/competitors to see what you might be able to find on them and then extrapolate creatively. Business research is more of an art than a science, so don't be afraid to make some logical leaps—and encourage your patron to do the same.

RESOURCES: COMPANY INFORMATION

Note: See also the relevant sections in chapter 2, "The Business Reference Resource (aka the Business Reference Database)."

This section will cover some free and fee-based resources where you can start your search for company information. The focus is on online resources, but keep in mind that a specialized directory or other print source may sometimes be your only option for finding anything. However, it's often best (and usually easiest) to start online in the hopes of getting the most current information available. Companies can hire, fire, or retitle executives, buy or sell subsidiaries, and change in other fairly fundamental ways faster than print sources can keep up with. Some print resources that you should familiarize yourself with, though, are included in this section.

Some free sources are listed here, but remember that "free" often comes with a catch, either in the form of advertising windows popping up or registration being required or some other form of distracting time sink. And don't forget that the time you spend digging has a cost, too. As the saying goes, time is money, so manage yours efficiently and know when it's time to step back and try another source or rethink your strategy altogether. If you're in a medium to large public or academic library, the reference stacks can hold a wealth of company information (among other things), if you're not afraid of digging a little. Please note that many of these titles have either a stand-alone online version or are available as part of various database packages. I've tried to note these where possible.

I've also broken out the resources by the kind of company information or functionality you'll primarily find in them (packaged profiles, directory information that can be exported, etc.) and tried to note when a resource covers both public and private or only public. Keep in mind that some of these resources provide lots of different kinds of content and functionality. And, while you can find some financial and stock market data in some of these resources, company financial resources are covered in chapter 5, "Company Finance," and stock market resources are covered in chapter 6, "Investment Research."

Hoover's (some free content; covers public and private companies)
www.hoovers.com

Hoover's was mentioned in chapter 2, but it's worth highlighting again here because as long as you don't mind putting up with some ads, the free version of Hoovers.com is a great starting point for company research. Many company profile databases will search only parent company names, so if you enter in the name of a subsidiary, you'll turn up empty-handed. Because you can do a keyword search across company names and descriptions in Hoover's, even if the patron is positive that Old Navy is the name of the parent company they want to research, you can quickly find it listed in the Gap Inc. profile and continue your searching from there. Starting your search in Hoover's may provide you with some initial clues that you can build upon when searching in other resources.

Company websites (free)
Find these using Google (use the advanced search if you're having trouble tracking down a company with a common name—you can use *not* to filter out terms that are cluttering up your results). Don't overlook the information that can be found on a company's website. While a public company's website will provide SEC filings and other investor information, even a private company's website can provide a wealth of information. Keep in mind that all of the information is coming from the perspective of the company itself and is only what they've decided to make available and/or highlight. Still not sure after looking through the company's website whether it's public or private? Keep an eye out for a "For Investors," "About Us," or similar link, which will indicate that the company is public, point you toward who the parent is, or provide other ownership clues.

International Directory of Company Histories (print and online)
www.gale.cengage.com

The hundreds of company profiles in the International Directory of Company Histories are an invaluable source of company information. Entries are three to five pages long and the series is up to over one hundred volumes with frequent updated entries added for companies that have undergone any major changes. If you're looking for a thorough overview of a company, this directory is a must. Many smaller companies are included, so it's worth checking to see what's in there. Note that this content is available online through the Business and Company Resource Center database (soon to be replaced by the Business Insights: Essential database) as well as Gale Directory Library.

International Directory of Business Biographies (IDBB; print and online)
www.referenceforbusiness.com/biography/

This directory is a great source of background information on the CEOs and other leaders of major companies. Even though this covers people more than companies themselves, the IDBB is a great resource to use to get additional insight into the business you're researching. A print version is available through St. James Press, although the link here points to a free version with the same content.

Thomas Register (online)
www.thomasnet.com
You may remember having seen the big green books that made up the thirty-four-volume set of the Thomas Register on your reference shelves, at least until they ceased publication with their one hundredth and final edition in 2006. Now if you want to know who makes what, you can check out ThomasNet. ThomasNet is easily browsed—or you can search by company name, product, or available CAD drawings. ThomasNet is a great source for information on industrial distributors and manufacturers and related services.

Manufacturing and Distribution USA
www.gale.cengage.com
Formed by the union of Manufacturing USA and Wholesale and Retail Trade USA, Manufacturing and Distribution USA from Gale Cengage Learning provides statistics on over 850 industries. Some state-specific titles may be available, too, such as Manufacturing Illinois, usually published locally.

A NOTE ABOUT ORGANIZATIONAL CHARTS

Sometimes a patron will ask for a company's organizational chart (or "org chart" for short). These are documents that illustrate the various positions, titles, and departments within a company and who reports to whom. Finding a ready-made org chart is not as easy as it might seem on the surface—these are generally considered proprietary. Companies aren't required to disclose their organizational structure, and in general they'd like to keep this kind of internal operations intelligence to themselves. You may be able to find an unofficial chart by searching for the terms *org chart* and [*company name*], but it may not be accurate or up to date. Some sites like CogMap (www.cogmap.com) offer tools to help you create org charts and offer example, unofficial, org charts to view. Some sites like the Conference Board (www.conference-board.org/publications/orgcharts/) and The Official Board (www.theofficialboard.com) offer org charts for a fee. There is also a (dated) book on org charts: *Organization Charts: Structures of 230 Businesses, Government Agencies, and Non-profit Organizations*, edited by Nick Sternberg and Scott Heil (Detroit: Gale Group, 2000). When faced with an org chart request, one thing you can do to help the patron is guide her to a company information database mentioned in chapter 2 or even simply to the company's website. You may be able to find at least some information about the key executives and other personnel and construct an unofficial org chart yourself. It may also be helpful to search in an article database for the company's name and terms like *organizational structure*. A Google trick that may yield an org chart example or two is to limit your search to the Microsoft PowerPoint format (you can do this in the File Types field of Google's advanced search screen [www.google.com/advanced_search] or you can add *filetype:ppt* to your [*company name*] *organizational chart* search).

COMPANY RANKINGS RESOURCES

Sometimes a company research question will involve a hunt for a ranked list of companies based on some kind of criteria such as sales or number of employees. Some of the databases noted in chapter 2 in the directory category might help you build some lists of your own through various screening strategies. And the following resources can also come in handy when you're looking for any kind of company ranking.

Business Rankings Annual (Gale Cengage Learning) (print and online)
www.gale.cengage.com
This well-indexed resource lists rankings of companies and industries and points you toward their original source (for example, World's Most Admired General Merchandisers as reported in *Fortune* magazine), and saves you from having to dig through all kinds of articles trying to find a published list. Business Rankings Annual is also available online through the Business and Company Resource Center. A sister publication is Gale's *Market Share Reporter*, which may provide you with additional data for comparison. Note that this content is available online through the Business and Company Resource Center database (soon to be replaced by the Business Insights: Essential database) as well as Gale Directory Library.

RDS TableBase (Gale Cengage Learning) (online only)
www.gale.cengage.com
See page 14 (chapter 2, "The Business Reference Resource [aka the Business Reference Database]"). This product is worth mentioning again because TableBase indexes articles contain ranked lists. As with Business Rankings Annual (see previous entry), you'll be pointed to the original source of the data and can then possibly track back to find even more information.

Dun & Bradstreet's Business Rankings (print)
Dun & Bradstreet publishes a number of directories. Their Business Rankings publication ranks public and private U.S. companies by sales volume and number of employees within the entire United States, within states, and within industry category by SIC code. It also ranks public companies by size and private/foreign-owned companies by size in separate sections.

Gary Price's List of Lists (online only)

www.specialissues.com/lol/

The List of Lists is a website pointing to ranked listings of companies, people, and resources all freely available on the Internet. Even though many of the lists pointed to are dated, this is a great place to look for clues about trade journals and special issues featuring ranked lists.

Rankings sources from the Library of Congress (online only)

www.loc.gov/rr/business/company/rankings.html

This handy site points you toward a number of the ranking sources listed here, as well as some special issues from journals and other industry-specific sources for rankings.

SOCIAL MEDIA RESOURCES

Another area that could have its own chapter or entire book devoted to it is the growing use of social media tools like Facebook, Twitter, LinkedIn, and Flickr for business research. Social media outlets can be especially useful sources of information on small, private companies. I won't go in depth on the mechanics of using social media for this kind of research, but I did want to make sure to highlight it in this chapter so that it is at least on your business reference radar.

Rutgers University Libraries has a great guide, "Urban Entrepreneurship" (http://libguides.rutgers.edu/content.php?pid=295160&sid=2423277), that highlights social media. FUMSI published a good article titled "Twitter for Business Intelligence" (http://web.fumsi.com/go/article/find/64010). If you search around in the information professional literature, you'll find a lot more. Scott Brown of the Social Information Group frequently covers this topic at library conferences and workshops (www.socialinformationgroup.com). Brown wrote "Social Media for Company Research: A Few of the Best Tools" (*Business Information Review*, vol. 28, no. 3, 2011). And you'll likely see this topic covered by other search professionals as well as in the popular press, as in an article from late 2011 in *Entrepreneur*, "How to Use Social Media for Research and Development" (www .entrepreneur.com/article/220812). You never know when a creative search in social media might help you find information on a small company or hit the business reference jackpot, so be sure to consider incorporating it into your strategy.

START MAKING SENSE!

■ Pick a favorite (or hated!) company and use it as your sample search in a database or print resource or two. Can't think of one? Where do you grocery shop? What kind of car do you drive?

What's your favorite national chain restaurant? What database company would you like to find out more about? Take note of what you can and can't find—were you looking for a private company in a database that only covers public companies? Were you searching for a subsidiary?

■ Can't find anything on a small, private company besides their website or a few sales estimates? Try to identify a similar company (ideally a public one) that you can find information on and creatively extrapolate.

■ Pick a company and determine where they are headquartered, then identify the major newspapers from that region. If you can access those publications from a database or through their websites, search around and see what kind of coverage they provide on your company.

4

INDUSTRY RESEARCH

NDUSTRY RESEARCH QUESTIONS are probably the most frequently encountered—and sometimes the most difficult—types of business reference questions a librarian or other researcher will face. Questions that start off as innocent requests for company information or a particular product will many times veer into the realm of industry research. Questions from all kinds of disciplines such as medicine, engineering, psychology, and science can often incorporate aspects of industry research, too.

You may have noticed that there are no chapters in this book devoted to any specific industry, such as real estate, retail, or telecommunications. The strategies outlined in this chapter should help you approach any industry that comes your way, whether it's a relatively defined industry made up of mostly public companies (e.g., airlines or autos) or a little more blurry and fragmented (e.g., bakeries, scrapbooking, or "the going out" market). Not only that, but becoming adept at industry research strategies will in turn make you a stronger researcher of company information, consumer information, international business information, and so on. Because industry research questions are the cornerstone of business reference and because many of the strategies highlighted in this section will also work for other areas of business research, this chapter may be the most important of this book.

Often, industry-related questions overlap with consumer research topics, so be sure to look at chapter 7, "Consumer Research and Marketing/Advertising," for more ideas. Also, many of the business statistics covered in chapter 8, "Business (and Other) Statistics," relate to various industries, so use that chapter in tandem with this one for additional strategies. And, if you'd like to be walked through some example industry reference questions, don't miss the "Industry" section of the Stumper appendix at the end of this book.

GETTING STARTED: INDUSTRY RESEARCH

I wish there were a simple, step-by-step method I could offer up for finding the exact industry data you're researching, for every industry, every time you were looking for it. But the straight truth is that this just isn't going to happen. Industry research is much more nuanced and, at times, much more complicated, than can be boiled down to any kind of formula.

If you're thinking that all this will involve quite a bit of flexibility, creativity, and tenacity on your part and the part of your patron, you're right! These traits are key to successful industry research. I was once helping a student work through an industry research assignment for a class when he looked at me and asked plaintively, "Aren't they asking us to do an awful lot of work?" I didn't know quite how to respond except to say, "Well, this is why consultants get paid a lot of money. And yes, it's an awful lot of work."

First and foremost, as with almost any kind of research, the key to industry research success is to constantly be on the lookout for clues. With that in mind, also be sure to take the following steps.

Define the Industry

Start off by clarifying the definition of the industry in question as best as you can. Defining what the patron is looking for when they say "cosmetics" or "solar energy" or "sports clothing" can help guide your industry information search. Don't forget to consider synonyms (e.g., *oil* or *petroleum*) as well as related broader and narrower terms (e.g., *gasoline* or *energy*). Depending on the industry you're dealing with, things can get tricky, either because the industry is made up of numerous small and private companies or the major players operate in multiple industries, or the industry is a subset of a larger industry—or, often, some combination of these factors. Don't get too hung up on very specific definitions or terminology just yet, but start a mental or actual list of keywords as you brainstorm ways to describe the industry in question.

Ask Yourself, "Who Cares?"

One question I often tell students to ask themselves when faced with an industry question is, "Who cares?" Not "who cares?" as in "this is for the birds," but "who cares?" as in "who might be out there who thinks about this stuff on a regular basis or is impacted by the things that go on related to this topic?" These can be industry associations, consumer groups, think tanks, and the like. Focus on identifying an association or other relevant group first (some tips on how to identify who cares are below in the "Resources" section) and then dig through their website, rather than spinning your wheels googling the same industry terms over and over again.

It may seem old-fashioned in these modern times, but one of the most powerful tools available to the business researcher is the telephone. Don't be afraid to pick it up and call someone at one of these places. If nothing else, these groups can serve as a sanity check and tell you whether the data you are looking for is even tracked. Often they can help you sift through the data you've already got or point you toward even better data.

Do be aware that many of these associations, think tanks, and other groups have an underlying agenda. Some will be touted as nonpartisan or independent, but more often than not, those that are left- or right-leaning will not come out and state this clearly. This is something to consider when dealing with any unfamiliar source of information, but especially so when you're essentially trolling the Internet for relevant groups.

Start Digging, and Then Dig Some More

Industry research is an area where thinking like an inspired, stubborn detective will come in especially handy. Prepare yourself—and your patron—for some digging and more digging and, not to harp on this, but to constantly be on the lookout for clues while doing so.

Where to dig, you ask? Many of the industry profile databases covered in chapter 2 will be a great source of information, so if your library or institution is lucky enough to subscribe to some of them, by all means take a look there for the industry in question. However, keep in mind that many packaged industry reports will not cover smaller niche industries, nor will they be as up to date in terms of market size and major players data as what you might find through an article search. So, even if you can find a nice, ready-made profile, you'll also likely want to supplement it by digging in article databases and online.

How to dig, you ask? Most important, do NOT start by trying to find the exact, very granular, very specific answer. Remember to parse out what is being looked for into broader categories and focus on those individual pieces of the puzzle, not the holy grail. More often than not, initiating a narrowly focused industry search will only cause you to spin your wheels in frustration. Even if your patron wants to know about the cupcake industry in Ann Arbor or about plus-size lingerie in Canada, start a little more broadly and keep in mind you may need to step back a few paces. Begin by looking for industry profiles on bakeries or articles on the rise in cupcake popularity, or about the general plus-size and the intimate apparel markets, and extrapolate from what you can find.

Along those same lines, remember that when it comes to article searching, less is more, so don't try to plug in every facet of your search all at once. As I mentioned in the beginning of the book, break the question into manageable chunks and approach each part individually before trying to home in on the sweet spot. Take advantage of advanced search features, such as opening your search up to "all text" or truncating a relevant keyword, and other tricks that may help you in your industry research struggles.

And don't discount the value of a simple online search using Google or another tool—just be creative with it and remember that the "less is more" tenet of article searching holds true and then some when you're on the open Internet. Keep the "who cares?" framework in mind and use a search engine to help you identify associations. Or plug in some of your industry keywords to see what might turn up. It's a great way to get a quick, smart start on the lingo, and you never know when you might hit the jackpot. Add terms like *association* or *organization* to your search or limit it to .org sites (especially if you keep running into .com sites that are trying to sell you something), and you may even find the Cupcake Association of Southeast Michigan or the Plus-Size Intimate Apparel Consumer Coalition based in Saskatchewan (neither of these groups is real, to my knowledge, but you never know with industry searching).

Pearl Gathering

You may have come across the term *pearl gathering* in relation to basic research tips. Essentially, you want to be on the lookout for how you can use the clues (or pearls) that you find along the way to help point you toward additional information (more pearls!). For example, if you do manage to track down an article that is close to the topic at hand, take a look at elements such as subject headings, and use those to point you toward additional articles. Or, take a look at the article's bibliography or footnotes and see if they point toward original sources of data—a study or an association, for example. One trick I often employ is to go to Google Scholar (http://scholar.google.com), a news database, or a website and do a quick search for a few relevant keywords to see what kinds of articles and papers turn up. If it's an academic paper, I'll look through the list of data sources or references and see if they can provide any leads for me to follow up on. If it's an article, I'll skim it to see if it references any relevant groups or studies. Sometimes you'll luck out and get a nugget or two of data, or at least a lead on something to track down. Or maybe you already have a few pearls to start with. Do you know some companies that operate within the industry you're researching? Take a known item like that into a company research database or into an article search and look for information on those companies; see if their industry is mentioned. These are probably habits you are already incorporating in your everyday research life, but it can be easy to forget the basics when faced with a snarly business reference question, especially a snarly industry question.

Another great way to use the open Internet when doing industry research is to try to identify a pathfinder or guide on the industry in question from an academic or public library. I often will go to Google (or another search engine) and type my industry keyword(s). Depending on the terminology, I may also include the word *industry* in the search and then also add the word *library* and limit the search to .edu sites. This will often point me to at least one or two academic libraries that have collected an assortment of databases and websites specific to the industry I'm looking for. For example, if you do a search for *"apparel industry" library site:.edu*, you'll find a number of guides, some of which may point you toward databases you already have access to but hadn't thought to check yet. You may have to sift through a few results, but the leads you end up with will be worth it. If you find yourself doing this often enough with specific industries that seem to be popular subjects in your library setting, consider "stealing" from here and there and pull together an awesome pathfinder of your own! You can even search for *"industry research" library site:.edu* and see what turns up. One guide that includes some step-by-step guidance comes from the University of Florida: http://businesslibrary.uflib.ufl.edu/industryresearch. The University of Florida also publishes a nice list of links to business school library sites. See if one of them has a guide to an industry you're interested in: http://businesslibrary.uflib.ufl.edu/businesslibraries.

Remember, the key to industry research is to be on the lookout for clues. Did you see a mention of a study? An association? A market size or definition? Take some of these clues that you find as you continue your digging and go back in for another article or report search until you feel like you've pursued every angle. As you hone your search (or help guide your patron's search) and continue to dig, you should start to see some clues that you can incorporate into your next search until you've finished digging.

Partner with Your Patron and Others

It's especially important to work with the patron to determine what they really want when you're dealing with an industry research question. It's also important to manage the expectations of the patron. Make sure to clarify as best you can what might and might not be out there and emphasize that to pull together a comprehensive industry overview requires a lot of digging (and/or a lot of money; packaged industry information takes a lot of time and analysis to compile—now you can see why!). Of course, the more familiar you become with the various industry resources available to you and with industry research in general, the better able you'll be to make these clarifications and recommendations. Prepare your patron to be flexible and not to turn up their nose at a report that may be on a related or broader industry and that doesn't necessarily focus on their specific industry. For example, industry reports on health and beauty can be useful to someone interested in cosmetics; an alternative energy industry report may work for someone looking at solar power; an apparel industry report might satisfy someone looking at sports clothing. These can be gold mines of clues and other info if the patron is willing to keep an open mind and approach the research creatively and with flexibility.

Don't be afraid to ask for help, either—think aloud and invite colleagues to brainstorm on some keywords or strategies. Tag-team business reference is not only more fun, it's also often more successful than slogging through a query alone. When all else fails (or better yet, before it does), take advantage of some of the groups listed in chapter 11, "Other Handy Business Reference Resources and Tips," and send out the bat signal to other business reference librarians for help!

Just know that the industry research process, perhaps more so than in any other area of business reference, will require communication with the patron and will also require of you the creativity and tenacity and patience that have been mentioned earlier throughout this book.

Keeping Track of It All

All this defining and digging and gathering of pearls/clues can leave your head spinning. I make it a point to recommend to any patron or team of students I'm working with on an industry research project to keep some kind of a research log. By consciously keeping track of their research process—the resources they used, the terms they searched for, the clues they found, and so on—they won't find themselves having to backtrack quite as much when they return the next day to look for more information. There's no "right" way to keep track of everything; it's really just a matter of personal preference. Some might want to handwrite everything in a spiral notebook, while others might want to e-mail themselves notes. The important thing is to do it. Those who heed your advice will thank you, and those who don't will be kicking themselves at some point down the industry research road.

Industry Research Summary

To sum things up, here are a few tips to keep in mind when undertaking any kind of industry research.

Put on your deerstalker and be prepared to look for clues everywhere
Define your industry and brainstorm descriptive keywords
Ask yourself, "Who cares?" to point you toward relevant industry and consumer groups that may have additional information.
Consider contacting an expert directly if you're feeling stuck.

Dig in: article databases, industry databases, and the open Internet.
Dig for: reports, articles, pathfinders, associations, trade journals,
or anything else that might provide some clues

Don't get tunnel vision and start your search too narrowly. Consider
tracking back to the original source of data if you find references
to studies or articles that cite additional data.

Don't re-create the industry research wheel—use an open Internet
search to identify an industry guide or pathfinder that might
point you toward databases and other useful sources.

Keep track of the clues and other search leads you find along the
way. If you end up with a lot of great stuff, consider building
pathfinders of your own and share the wealth.

Talk to your coworkers and run your question by them, or ask for
help from the business reference community at large.

UNDERSTANDING SIC, NAICS, AND OTHER INDUSTRY CODES

NAICS (rhymes with *snakes*) and SIC (pronounced *S-I-C*) codes can be useful tools when doing research on an industry or looking into a company's competitors. Essentially, the North American Industry Classification Codes (NAICS) and the Standard Industrial Classification System (SIC) codes broadly classify the industry areas in which a company operates.

NAICS were developed in 1997 and were intended to supersede the 1987 SIC codes. NAICS had more room to include the emerging information and technical sectors as well as other industry changes. But, like any new idea, the new codes took some time to catch on and SIC codes are still in use in many proprietary databases and other systems. If you're going to work with industry codes, it's good to be aware of both the SIC codes and NAICS classification so that you can be ready for anything.

And, just to keep you on your toes, there are other general classification systems out there as well as more specialized ones. Some databases incorporate their own codes and classifications in addition to using NAICS and/or SIC codes. NAICS and SIC just happen to be the closest to universal schemes than any others you're likely to come across in the typical business reference setting. And while not all industry resources utilize NAICS, SIC, or other codes in their indexing, being aware of these classification systems can help you make best use of those that do.

I find that the quickest way to look up SIC and NAICS classifications is to use the U.S. Census correspondence tables: www.census.gov/epcd/www/naicstab .htm. In a pinch, just google *NAICS SIC* and you'll be pointed toward that page. I also like the Census's Industry Statistics Sampler (http://www.census.gov/econ/ industry/), which is fairly easy to search and provides some more detailed information on the NAICS definitions as well as linking to relevant data by NAICS code.

Some SIC/NAICS Examples

A helpful analogy toward understanding NAICS vs. SIC codes is the relationship between the Library of Congress Classification system and the Dewey Decimal Classification. Just as NAICS were developed to expand upon the existing SIC structure and to open up room for new industries, so too was LC developed to expand upon the Dewey system and make room for non-Western-focused coverage and new topics as well. Also, just as Dewey has its decimal points and items are broadly categorized by the hundreds (e.g., 700 The Arts) and LC has its letters (e.g., N—FINE ARTS), SIC and NAICS also get more granular the more you drill down. And, just as LC and Dewey codes are just one tool that you can use to identify books, industry codes are just one tool for use in industry research.

Here is an example for the book *Middlemarch* (give or take some local cataloging issues):

Middlemarch

■ Library of Congress call number: PR4662 .A1
■ Dewey call number: 823 E42MIB1956

Here is an example for a book on marketing to mothers:

Trillion-Dollar Moms: Marketing to a New Generation of Mothers

■ Library of Congress call number: HF5415.33.U6 B35 2005
■ Dewey call number: 658.830852 B155t2005

So: same books, just different "codes." And you'd need to know which kind of library you were in to know which code to use. Similarly, you can look at the same industry and see different codes describing it. Here are the codes for frozen fruits and vegetables manufacturing (keep in mind that, unlike book titles, the descriptions can vary between codes):

Frozen fruits, fruit juices, and vegetables, manufacturing

■ NAICS code: 311411 (31–33 is "Manufacturing" and 311 is "Food Manufacturing")
■ SIC code: 2037 (20 is "Food and kindred products" manufacturing)

Full-Service Restaurants

■ NAICS code: 722111 (722 is "Food Services and Drinking Places")
■ SIC code: 5812 (58 is "Eating and drinking places")

Some Caveats and Tips for Dealing with SIC/NAICS Codes

Generally, databases will indicate a primary code to identify the company's main area of business and sometimes use additional codes to indicate other areas of activity, so a company can have more than one SIC or NAICS code. Also, it's never really been clear to me just how exactly the codes get assigned—do the companies just pick codes themselves and then report them along with other information? Do the database companies assign codes? With this in mind, it's important to understand that using SIC/NAICS codes will not necessarily produce an exhaustive, comprehensive list of an industry's players (at least not according to how you've defined things), so don't get too excited just because you've found what appears to be a relevant code or two. For example, one database might classify Starbucks as a "limited service restaurant" (NAICS 722211) and classify Dunkin' Donuts as a "baked goods store"—so if you search for one or the other, you still won't end up with a complete list of coffee shops. Not to mention that if you search for *coffee shops* in the aforementioned Industry Statistics Sampler, you'll be pointed to a code for "snack and nonalcoholic beverage bars" (NAICS 722213). Also, since companies can do more than one thing (sell more than one type of product, manufacture more than one type of good), you can expect to run into issues related to that. Also, expect to encounter the dreaded "Other" (other information services) or "Miscellaneous" (miscellaneous manufacturing) categories when dealing with industry classification systems. Depending on how precise you need to be in identifying relevant companies or business counts, make use of these codes with some caution and skepticism.

Remember that these codes are just one of many industry research tools and not every industry has a related code, nor do the codes tell you everything even when you can find one.

RESOURCES: INDUSTRY INFORMATION
Note: See also the relevant sections in chapter 2, "The Business Reference Resource (aka the Business Reference Database)."

Industry report aggregator sites
Sites such as MarketResearch.com and ResearchandMarkets.com are highlighted here because they will often turn up in an industry research scenario. These kinds of sites and the shiny, packaged reports they are reselling are easily found by patrons doing an open Internet search, and the reports sound like they cover exactly what your patrons are looking for (e.g., "The U.S. Market for Golf Equipment"). If a patron can afford to purchase these reports and appears to be headed in that direction, encourage them to first ask the publishers to send a sample of the data to confirm that it covers what they need. Better yet, encourage your patrons to try out some of the industry research tips mentioned earlier in this chapter to see if they can find comparable (or even better) data themselves. If the patrons are students doing industry research as part of an assignment, I would almost always deter them from purchasing these kinds of reports. They are already paying tuition, and it is not likely their professor intended for them to buy data as part of the assignment. Most aggregator sites will allow some type of free registration. Once

you're registered you can access the abstracts of many reports and sometimes even find bits and pieces of industry information. This is also a good place for determining which research companies focus on particular industries, and you can then go to their site to see if it has additional information.

Encyclopedia of American Industries (Grey House Publishing/Gale Cengage Learning)
www.gale.cengage.com

The Encyclopedia of American Industries is a great starting point for industry research. Each industry profile provides an overview of that industry's structure, history, development, leaders, and more. Broken out by SIC code, in the print version volume 1 covers manufacturing industries and volume 2 covers service and nonmanufacturing industries. Note that this content is available online through the Business and Company Resource Center database (soon to be replaced by the Business Insights: Essential database) as well as Gale Directory Library.

Encyclopedia of Emerging Industries (Grey House Publishing/Gale Cengage Learning)
www.gale.cengage.com

This is a companion to the Encyclopedia of American Industries and focuses on over one hundred "new" industries such as extreme sports, charter schools, smart cards, and even pet services. It is an excellent place to turn for many of those hard-to-categorize industries that patrons are often researching. Note that this content is available online through the Business and Company Resource Center database (soon to be replaced by the Business Insights: Essential database) as well as Gale Directory Library.

GlobalEdge Industry Profiles
http://globaledge.msu.edu/industries/

Michigan State University's GlobalEdge project has some nice overviews of a number of industries. Profiles include links to related online resources such as industry associations as well as to information on risk related to the industry and lists of top companies around the world in each industry.

Vault Industry Overviews (free registration required)
www.vault.com/wps/portal/usa/industries/

Vault is a fairly well-known business career resource—they publish a number of guides on various industries that are geared toward a job-seeking audience. Their online site points to a lot of fee-based material, but there are some useful industry profiles, ranked lists, and other resources here if you look carefully.

Harvard Business School Baker Library Industry Overview Index
www.library.hbs.edu/guides/#industry/

Covering the holdings of Harvard Business School's Baker Library, this is a great site if you're trying to identify specific industry information resources. Check out trade journals in the specific industry area you're researching and see if they publish special reports (sometimes these are freely available online).

Economic Census
www.census.gov/econ/census/
While I wouldn't necessarily start my industry research here, the Economic Census is a vast source of industry information. So vast, in fact, that an entire guide has been written to help users weed through the overwhelming amount of data (*Industry Research Using the Economic Census: How to Find It, How to Use It,* by Jennifer C. Boettcher and Leonard M. Gaines [Westport, CT: Greenwood Press, 2004]). The Economic Census is done only every five years, so there are a number of other reports published during the off years (although the data is not always posted immediately), including the "Annual Survey of Manufacturers," the "Annual Retail Trade Survey" (see the following entry), and others.

Survey of Manufacturers and Annual Retail Trade Survey
www.census.gov/main/www/a2z/E/#E411/
Browse through the Economic Data and Information section of the A-to-Z subject guide of the U.S. Census for more resources, including the "Survey of Manufacturers" and the "Annual Retail Trade Survey".

Library of Congress's BRS Assists Industry Surveys
www.loc.gov/rr/business/assists/indsur.html
This bibliography from the Business Reference Services division of the Library of Congress points to a number of titles featured here as well as other sites for industry information.

IN ADDITION TO SEARCHING article databases, consider going straight to the websites of usual suspects such as Bloomberg *Businessweek* or *Fortune* and drilling down, looking for special reports related to your industry. Often there is content online that doesn't turn up in a database search. If you can put up with the ads and the ubiquitous false leads to subscriber-only content, you can often strike gold. If you do get pointed to subscriber-only content, double-check to see whether your library has access. Did I mention that you usually have to dig for industry information?

Print Resources for Industry Research
Note: Don't forget to check your catalog (or the catalog of another library with a larger business collection) to see what kinds of monographs on the topic of your industry are available. Also, as of the writing of this book, some of the print resources listed below are being reviewed by their publishers and may at some point be dropped in favor of online content only.

Standard & Poor's Industry Surveys

Many libraries who don't subscribe to the full NetAdvantage database do still have print versions of the *Industry Surveys* on their reference shelves (usually in three large binders). Industries covered include autos and auto parts, broadcasting and cable, computer networking, health care products and supplies, and restaurants. If you have access to the print version of the *Industry Surveys*, the back cover of each lists all the industries in the set.

Mergent's Industry Review (formerly Moody's Industry Review)

www.mergent.com/productsServices-print-industryReview.html

This source covers approximately 140 industry groups and includes lists of top-ranked companies within each industry according to key financial and investment criteria, and comparative financial statistics such as earnings per share and stock price range. Growth rates for top companies within each industry are also included.

Value Line Investment Survey

www.valueline.com

See page 20 (chapter 2, "The Business Reference Resource [aka the Business Reference Database]"). The print version of Value Line offers the same short overviews of a number of industry sectors included in the online version.

Plunkett Research Almanacs

www.plunkettresearch.com/HowtoBuy/IndustryList/tabid/105/
Default.aspx

See page 18 (chapter 2, "The Business Reference Resource [aka the Business Reference Database]"). Many libraries purchase only select print titles of these almanacs.

START MAKING SENSE!

- Take a look at your collection (online and print) to familiarize yourself with some of the industry research resources you may have.
- Identify a database or free online resource or print reference source and browse through its industry offerings. Take note of what you can and can't find and the different ways the same industries can be described using different terminology.
- Continue to flex your industry research muscles by taking your search into an article database or open Internet search—or both. Identify some related industry associations or trade journals. See

if you can find some tidbits of data related to the size of the industry you're looking into or note some of the major players.
■ Identify and then browse through some of the industry research guides published by business and other libraries. Take note of what stands out and consider building some of your own path-finders.

5

COMPANY FINANCE

YOU DON'T NEED to be a CPA (certified public accountant) or have advanced corporate finance skills to understand a little bit about the basics of company finance. Sometimes a company information question will focus on a company's financials; that is, how much money they make and how much money they spend doing so. All companies track this information internally, and publicly traded companies are required to report some of this information to their shareholders (and everybody else) in the form of regulated accounting documents. I'm no expert or even a hobbyist when it comes to financial topics, but this chapter should give you an idea of what is—and isn't—out there and why the information might be requested. Remember, it's not your job to analyze and interpret a balance sheet or other financial data but to point your patrons toward resources for finding this information.

This chapter will also cover how to use a basic understanding of company finance to help you creatively extrapolate from the data you find when you're struggling with a company or an industry that you can't seem to find anything else on.

As I've mentioned, it is generally easier to find information on publicly traded companies than private ones. This is true and then some for financial data. This is due, in part, to SEC rules that regulate public companies. Two SEC regulations in particular, the Securities Exchange laws of 1933–34 and the Sarbanes-Oxley Act of 2002, can help give this complicated topic some context.

Among other laws, public companies are regulated by the Securities Exchange laws of 1933–34. Previous to the Great Crash of 1929, there was little to no federal regulation of the securities market. Companies were not held to any standard for disclosure of their business activities. Congress passed the Securities Act of 1933 and the Securities Exchange Act of 1934 to restore consumer confidence in the market. These laws essentially require companies that offer the public the ability to invest in them to be truthful about their business and its finances and about the risks involved in investing. These laws also require that people who trade and sell securities must also be honest and put investors' interests first. In other words, companies that take money from investors can't say they do one thing but actually do another, and they have to file documentation with the SEC to prove that they're complying with these rules. This was the standard for decades until the Sarbanes-Oxley Act of 2002.

Sarbanes-Oxley was passed in response to the Enron, Worldcom, and numerous other corporate accounting scandals. While these companies were filing their required documentation with the SEC and seemingly following the law, many of them were also practicing what is sometimes referred to as "creative accounting" or "earnings management" and in effect doctoring their numbers. When this doctoring came to light, many of these corporate leaders claimed that it was the accountants who were at fault. Sarbanes-Oxley essentially requires that CEOs and other company managers sign off on the information that is released to shareholders. No longer can they claim ignorance when it comes to their own company finances.

Of course, the reality of accounting, corporate finance, and securities regulation is a lot more complicated than this, and this is simply my humble attempt at understanding some fairly complex financial and legal issues. I hope these explanations provide at least a little insight. If you're looking for more, many of the resources below have some additional information, as do some of the educational websites that are referred to in chapter 6, "Investment Research."

GETTING STARTED: COMPANY FINANCE

The trick to answering company finance questions is first to determine what kind of numbers can be found and then figuring out what can be done with those numbers. The following are a few examples of where company financial and other information can be found.

Companies produce a number of reports, statements, filings, and other documents that provide financial information. These, in turn, are reviewed and analyzed by investors, management, lenders, and others interested in the financial stability or potential profitability of the company. A few that are helpful to familiarize yourself with include the following. (Some of these definitions come from the Investopedia.com website, a useful resource if you'd like to examine any of these further.)

> The *balance sheet* gives investors a general overview of a company's financial health. That is, it tells investors exactly what a company owns (assets) and who it owes (liabilities).
>
> The *income statement* tells investors about the company's profits and losses for a specific time period. Consider it a snapshot of a company's performance during any one given time period or how good they are at making money.
>
> Many of the items on the *cash flow statement* are also found in either the income statement or the balance sheet, but here they're arranged to highlight the cash generated and how it relates to reported earnings. The cash flow statement shows how a company pays for their operations and how they are planning their spending for future growth (to some extent).
>
> The *annual report to shareholders (ARS)* is more than just a financial statement. It provides a sort of year-in-review-and-where-we're-heading update intended for company investors. The annual report tends to be a glossy magazine–like report, with a letter to shareholders from the CEO, among other descriptions of the company's performance and other information. Annual reports usually focus less on financial information than their SEC-filed 10K (see below) counterpart.
>
> The *10K* is the form number for the SEC-filed version of the annual report. It's sometimes referred to as the annual report, but they are two separate documents, although some of the information will overlap and sometimes companies will opt to publish only the 10K. The 10K is a no-frills, text-and-numbers only document that provides a lot of information on the financial and business health of a company. Generally, companies need to file their 10K with the SEC within three months of the end of their fiscal year.
>
> The *proxy statement (14-A)* is an SEC filing that contains biographical and compensation information on officers of the company. Proxy statements are sent out to shareholders in advance of meetings so that they can be informed of what's going on at the managerial level.

There are many other filings, including variations of the 14-A, quarterly statements, and other financial documents, but the above descriptions give some idea of what's out there. The federal disclosure requirements are not set in stone, and changes to the regulations can occur, so keep an eye out on the SEC page or pay attention to the business news.

Private/Subsidiary Company Financials and Other Considerations

Unlike public companies, the information you can find on private companies, subsidiaries, or divisions leans more toward the anecdotal than to detailed financial reports. Some directories do give basic financial figures such as estimated revenue, but most private company or subsidiary information is gained from literature searches of local newspapers, magazines, newsletters, wire services, and trade journals. So dig, dig, dig, but don't count on finding detailed financial data.

It's worth mentioning here that when it comes to researching private companies, the name Dun & Bradstreet often comes up. This may be because they publish the D&B Million Dollar Database (which contains private companies and subsidiaries), so their name is associated with the topic. They also publish Dun & Bradstreet Credit Reports and other profiles that they sell for a fee. You'll see these offered for sale on Hoovers.com (which D&B owns) and some other sites. It's important to keep in mind that these reports usually only provide credit/payment information (essentially whether that company has paid its bills, to help you determine whether to lend them money), not necessarily financials or much in-depth data on the company. You'll often have someone demanding a D&B report, though, because they've been looking all over for information on a private company and have come across mention of these handy reports and thinks that their search is over. Remember, if it seems too good to be true . . .

Some of the tips in the next section give additional ideas on how to deal with private company analysis.

Industry and Financial Ratios

Industry and financial ratios can help you determine how well a company is performing compared to its peers. They can be complicated, since they are based on numerous financial and other data points, but they are worth noting briefly here.

Financial ratios are generally calculated using numbers from a company's financial statements. Depending on which numbers you're dividing, you can get a cursory look at a company's financial stability, its efficiency overall, its profits, and some future indicators of growth. If you average out these numbers across companies in the same industry, you can derive industry ratios. Patrons will often want a source that provides industry ratios so that they can do these comparisons without having to calculate industry figures themselves.

Common size analysis is a way of translating a company's financial statement into percentages so that it shows trends and can be compared to other companies, even if the company in question is much larger or smaller. For example, gross profit or cost of goods sold can be calculated as a percentage of total revenues and give an indication of how much is being spent to produce versus how much profit is left over. In other words, if Company A shows that they're spending only 10 percent of their total revenues to produce their products versus Company B's spending 50 percent, you might want to take a look into either how Company A manages to spend so little or why Company B spends so much.

This kind of analysis veers into the realm of requiring a corporate finance degree to understand, but having an idea of the basics behind the calculations and why someone would want them will give you a better idea of what sources to turn to and how to advise a patron in her research steps. Keep in mind that the goal of this book is not to teach you highly specialized financial analysis skills, but to make you aware of some of these processes and the resources where you can further edify yourself if you so choose.

If you or your patron prefer to avoid this kind of number crunching, there are other strategies to determine how a company is performing within an industry. One thing you can do is search for articles that include terms such as *benchmarking* or *best practice*. Find trade journals related to your industry to see who is highlighted and try looking for a list of companies ranked within an industry using some of the resources mentioned in chapter 3.

RESOURCES: COMPANY FINANCE
Note: See also the relevant sections in chapter 2, "The Business Reference Resource (aka the Business Reference Database)."

Remember—in most cases, you're going to find detailed financials only for publicly traded parent companies (and even those numbers might not be broken out in as much detail as your patron is hoping for). Most of these resources do not cover private companies. Some of these resources don't cover specific companies at all but provide definitions and explanations related to company finance topics.

Securities and Exchange Commission (SEC) (free online; primarily public companies)
www.sec.gov
The SEC makes sure that companies give the public basic facts about their business operations in order that everyone has information upon which to base investment decisions. Their website offers quite a bit of educational material, too, and even has a section specifically targeting librarians that is worth reviewing. EDGAR, the SEC's Electronic Data Gathering, Analysis, and Retrieval system, is the database you can use on the SEC website to find most of the various company filings going back about ten years. (SEC filings are included in many of the databases discussed in chapters 2 and 3.) Also, many websites offer the ability to search SEC filings and then charge you to access them. EDGAR access is free, although you may find that you prefer the search functionality of another product to access filings.

AnnualReports.com
This site provides quick access to a number of company reports. You can search by exchange or by industry or sector.

Campbell R. Harvey's Hypertextual Finance Glossary

www.duke.edu/~charvey/Classes/wpg/glossary.htm

This site's use of the term *hypertextual* always amuses me, but if you look beyond the clunky name there is a wealth of information here. This is a great place to look for a quick definition of a financial term you've never heard of or to quickly check an acronym. Since many of the definitions themselves are composed of difficult-to-understand financial terms, it's useful that these terms are themselves linked. For easier navigation of this site, get used to doing a "Find on page" search for the term you're looking for; otherwise you'll be doing a lot of hunting and scrolling.

Wachowicz's Web World

http://web.utk.edu/~jwachowi/wacho_world.html

Billed as "Websites for the Discerning Finance Student," you'll find a wide assortment of finance-related websites arranged in categories linked to *Fundamentals of Financial Management*, a textbook by John Wachowicz and James Van Horne. This isn't a site I'd use to answer a reference question, but rather to browse through to see where it leads. The site at first glance doesn't look very sophisticated, but it is frequently updated and provides links to relevant journals, business school rankings, podcasts, and more.

DON'T FORGET THE COMPANY'S website. Many public companies link their annual reports and SEC filings under an "Investor Relations" section on their website. Some private companies may give out a select few financials, but again, don't get your hopes up.

Websites such as Yahoo! Finance, Google Finance, and MSN Money are discussed in chapter 6, "Investment Research," but they are also often a quick and easy way to get at company financials, or to some explanations of company financial terms and topics.

RESOURCES: COMPANY AND INDUSTRY RATIOS

Financial Ratios Guide

www.anderson.ucla.edu/x14416.xml

The Anderson School of Management at UCLA has a great business topics guide. If you search the page for *financial ratios*, you'll be pointed toward where to find ratios by company and by industry as well as some handy explanations of ratios. They've also created guides to finding specific ratios: www.anderson.ucla .edu/x14413.xml (for industries) and www.anderson.ucla.edu/x14414.xml (for companies).

Almanac of Business and Industrial Financial Ratios

www.cchgroup.com/webapp/

This title, also known as "the Troy Almanac" after its author, Leo Troy, lists twenty-two financial and operating ratios for about 160 industries. Statistics are based on corporate activity during the latest year for which figures from IRS tax returns are published, so they are usually about three years old. The appendix lists almanac classification numbers and their corresponding SIC numbers.

Industry Norms and Key Business Ratios

Published by Dun & Bradstreet, the Industry Norms and Key Business Ratios product reports fourteen ratios for more than eight hundred SIC categories. Data is reported for median, upper, and lower quartiles. It includes balance sheet data reported in both dollars and percentages for each industry category, and is based on reports for over one million private and public companies in the D&B database.

Risk Management Association (RMA) Annual Statement Studies

www.rmahq.org/tools-publications/publications/annual
-statement-studies/

This core resource for industry ratios and benchmarks is from RMA, a banking organization (Risk Management Association, formerly Robert Morris Associates). It's arranged by NAICS code, with breakdowns by assets and sales size of companies in an industry. Individual NAICS profiles can be found online through the OneSource database. The print version contains some tips for how to read the data and also includes a brief overview of financial ratios.

BizStats

www.bizstats.com

This site offers a quick way to pick a particular industry, input a ballpark revenue number, and then see a quick common-size analysis chart. Scroll down and look at some of the other tables they provide. BizStats compiles raw statistical data from numerous sources, performs computations, and edits the information for the most meaningful statistics. They have a useful explanation of their methodology. While this kind of analysis is never exact, and it's also not clear how up to date the information is on all of the charts, it's worth a look. BizStats is owned by the Brandow Company and a fee-based version of this data and additional industry trend reports are available through their BizMiner product, mentioned in chapter 10, Small Business.

FINALLY, FOR MORE EXPLANATIONS on ratios, take a look at the websites listed below. These go into better detail and give some good examples:

Common Size Financial Statements: www.netmba.com/finance/
    statements/common-size/
Financial Calculator: www.bankrate.com/brm/news/biz/bizcalcs/
    ratiocalcs.asp

START MAKING SENSE!

- Check out the SEC's website and search for a company or two in the EDGAR database.
- Find a company's 10K from EDGAR and its annual report from the company website and compare.
- Pick a private company and see what kind of financial information you can find on it. Can you find a similar public company and creatively extrapolate?
- Skip ahead to chapter 6, "Investment Research," to see what kinds of education sites are listed. Most will focus on investing, but many cover basic financial explanations as well.
- Pick an industry in some of the ratio resources and take a look at the kind of information you can glean from those sources.

6

INVESTMENT RESEARCH

WHILE EXPLAINING THE ins and outs of Wall Street is beyond the scope of this book, the stock market and other investment arenas are a large part of the business reference landscape. This chapter provides a general overview of many of the topics you can expect to run across in this area. More important, I'll point out some nice guides where you or your patrons can find further explanations from people and organizations more versed in this complex topic than I am.

You'll find that you can get some of the same basic stock data in a lot of places for free online, but if you want to get historical prices or find defunct companies, you'll have to dig a little. In general, you'll find yourself turning toward some sources that you like to use best for quick searches and perhaps others for more in-depth questions. Being aware of the free resources as well as the fee-based databases your library might subscribe to and what kind of information you can—and can't—find in them will allow you to better assist your patrons.

This chapter also briefly touches upon other investment-related topics including bonds, mutual funds, commodities and futures, historical stock and bond data, and socially responsible investing.

INVESTOR EDUCATION SITES

Note: See also the relevant sections in chapter 2, "The Business Reference Resource (aka the Business Reference Database)."

Investor's Clearinghouse

www.investoreducation.org

The Investor's Clearinghouse offers reports and other information on consumer finance issues such as compulsive buying, senior investment fraud, retirement savings, and home equities. This site is produced by the Alliance for Investor Education, a nonprofit group comprising finance-related associations and other groups and is advised by the Federal Trade Commission, the Board of Governors of the Federal Reserve System, the Securities and Exchange Commission's Office of Investor Education and Assistance, and other reputable investment-related organizations. RSS feeds are available and highlight news and services offered by the members and advisors of the Alliance for Investor Education.

Path to Investing

www.pathtoinvesting.org

Path to Investing is also an objective, investor education website. It is managed by the Foundation for Investor Education. Path to Investing features what they call "guided trips," where industry experts write on topics such as bond investment, evaluating risk and return, and understanding home ownership. The core content breaks out topics such as investment goals, investing essentials, and how the markets work. A stock market simulation game called "Investor Challenge" is also included.

Investorwords.com

www.investorwords.com

Wondering what a structured note is, or can't remember the difference between *book value* and *net worth*? Investorwords.com is a handy place to look up a quick investment term. It's a commercial site, but they're pretty tame with the ads and pop-ups. Investorwords.com also features a stock research tool, which they run through their Investorguide.com site. (For more definitions, see also Campbell R. Harvey's Hypertextual Finance Glossary mentioned in chapter 5, "Company Finance.")

Stock Basics from Investopedia.com

www.investopedia.com/university/stocks/

A good place to learn the basics of stocks, from what they are to how they're traded.

How the Stock Market Works from How Stuff Works

http://money.howstuffworks.com/stock.htm

Another good site for getting a basic overview of the stock market.

Motley Fool's Fool School
www.fool.com/school.htm
This is a great site for you and your patrons to learn a little about investing and some of the various markets.

Money Chimp
www.moneychimp.com
This is a fun site that has some great overviews of the stock market, plus other financial and economic topics. My favorite feature is their "Chimp-a-go-go," which you can click to learn something random every day.

CNNMoney
http://money.cnn.com
Billing itself as the "Internet Home of Fortune and Money" magazine, among others, the CNNMoney site covers all the markets and provides numerous tutorials and overviews of finance-related topics.

INVESTING PUBLICATIONS

Sometimes browsing through a newspaper or journal that is focused on the markets can provide some edification as well as information. These are just a few of the more well-known publications in this area.

Barron's
http://online.barrons.com/home-page
Barron's is owned by Dow Jones and is part of the Wall Street Journal Digital Network. Their site provides news and analysis on the stock market as well as some investing ideas and other reports.

Bloomberg Businessweek
www.businessweek.com
Businessweek, now owned by Bloomberg, has a strong focus on the global markets.

Institutional Investor
www.institutionalinvestor.com
Many of the publications listed here focus on the individual investor to some extent. *Institutional Investor* focuses on the investment industry itself and provides rankings of money managers and other players in this sector as well as other international finance related topics.

Kiplinger's
www.kiplingers.com
Offers some overviews of investing as well as guides and other consumer-friendly financial advice.

New York Times
www.nytimes.com
The *New York Times*' business section as well as their Dealbook report provide excellent coverage of Wall Street and corporate America.

Wall Street Journal
www.wsj.com
While the *Wall Street Journal* certainly covers more than just investing news, it's worth noting here as a reminder that patrons may wish to consult the site for quick information on the stock markets and related information.

SOURCES OF STOCK INFORMATION

You can get free stock price information from a number of online sources, often going back quite a number of years. Some of these "free" sources will point to additional fee-based information, or you may find that you like some more than others due to their interface, lack of pop-up ads, historical coverage, ability to export to Microsoft Excel, and so on. Try a few to see which ones work the best for you. Keep in mind that all publicly traded companies have what are known as *ticker symbols* (from the ticker tape that was generated in print back in the early days of stock exchanges). These are one-, two-, three-, and sometimes four- or five-letter codes that are a company's unique identifier on a particular exchange. Most stock price resources have a ticker symbol search field. It's often best to have the ticker at hand to quickly pinpoint the company you're looking for, as well as to make sure you're looking at the correct company and not one with a similar name.

Morningstar (some free content)
www.morningstar.com
See page 18 (chapter 2, "The Business Reference Resource [aka the Business Reference Database]"). Morningstar is worth highlighting here again because of their focus on investment information. Morningstar covers a number of stocks and provides insight and analysis on their performance.

S&P's NetAdvantage Stock Reports
See page 19 (chapter 2, "The Business Reference Resource [aka the Business Reference Database]"). Standard & Poor's NetAdvantage includes Stock Reports for publicly traded companies.

Value Line (some free content)
www.valueline.com
See page 20 (chapter 2, "The Business Reference Resource [aka the Business Reference Database]"). Value Line has also been mentioned previously. It's products are common in most public and some academic library settings and are used by personal investors and company researchers alike because of their

proprietary rankings, ratings, and analysis. It's a huge resource for many investors and covers about 135 large public companies in seven or eight industries every week. A supplement covers about two thousand additional smaller companies.

Yahoo! Finance (free)
http://finance.yahoo.com
Yahoo! Finance is also mentioned in the company information section. It's a fairly straightforward site to turn to for easy-to-manipulate stock information, including historical coverage (for non-defunct companies) and the ability to compare across companies and/or indexes. There are additional features like tutorials on personal finance and the stock market.

BigCharts (free)
http://bigcharts.marketwatch.com
BigCharts offers company and industry information, interactive charts and news services, and historical quotes (for nondefunct companies). This site also offers lists of the best and worst performing industries based on stock price percent changes. It is a great free resource for building comparative charts of stocks and indexes.

Zacks Investment Research (some free content)
www.zacks.com
Zacks pulls together data feeds and printed research reports on over 10,000 companies from over 185 brokerage firms. They also record over 25,000 earnings estimate revisions and changes in broker recommendations weekly.

Bloomberg (some free content)
www.bloomberg.com
Bloomberg was founded and is still majority-owned (as of this writing) by New York City Mayor Michael Bloomberg. It provides financial news and data through its proprietary, stand-alone Bloomberg Terminal. Full access to Bloomberg data offers coverage of almost every kind of financial data out there, not just stock information. The website provides some basic info.

SOURCES OF STOCK AND COMMODITY EXCHANGE INFORMATION

Exchanges are entities that provide a place for stocks and commodities to be bought, sold, and otherwise traded. Check out some of the previous investor education sites for more explanation and background.

Stock and Commodity Exchanges Research Guide
http://libguides.rutgers.edu/stocks/
This site from Rutgers University lists stock and commodity exchanges worldwide (including those dealing in futures, options, and derivatives) as well as sources for market and stock prices and reports.

INDIVIDUAL EXCHANGES AND INDEXES also have information on their sites. Here are some examples.

New York Stock Exchange: www.nyse.com/home.html
Standard & Poor's indexes: www.standardandpoors.com
Russell U.S. Equity Indexes: www.russell.com/us/indexes/us/default.asp

SOURCES OF INITIAL PUBLIC OFFERINGS (IPO) INFORMATION

IPO Basics from Investopedia.com
www.investopedia.com/university/ipo/
Start here to learn about IPOs and why they're the focus of many investors.

How IPOs Work from How Stuff Works
http://money.howstuffworks.com/ipo.htm
Another useful overview of IPOs, including why companies have them, what happens on the day of an IPO, drawbacks to IPOs, and an interesting recap of Google's IPO.

Hoover's Online IPO Central
www.hoovers.com/global/ipoc/
IPO Central covers U.S. companies that have recently gone public or filed to go public. This service links the user to a subset of entries from the Hoover's Online site and to S-1 filings from EDGAR Online. Companies covered include those that initially filed with the SEC on or after May 6, 1996, the first day that all U.S. companies were required to file electronically. Listings are removed from IPO Central approximately six months after they have begun trading on a stock exchange.

Yahoo! IPOs
http://biz.yahoo.com/ipo/
A quick snapshot of best- and worst-performing IPOs, plus easy-to-navigate lists and other data.

SOURCES OF BOND INFORMATION AND EDUCATION

A bond can be considered a sort of IOU for a loan that has been provided at a certain interest rate to a company, a municipality, a government, or other entity (usually referred to as an *issuer*), which is due to be paid back at a certain time (the bond's *maturity*) to the respective bond holder (the *lender*). Companies can have bond ratings and these are indications of how well the banks think they can pay back their loans. The three major credit rating agencies (the companies that assign the ratings) that you'll come across are Standard & Poor's, Moody's, and Fitch. Bonds are a little bit beyond the scope of this chapter, but the overview from How Stuff Works (http://money.howstuffworks.com/question723.htm) has a little more info. And the Wikipedia entry "Bond Credit Ratings" (http://en.wikipedia .org/wiki/Bond_credit_rating) is fairly helpful.

When it comes to bonds, patrons are often looking for ratings of specific companies, often over time. Harvard's Baker Library points out a number of databases that contain some kind of ratings information (www.library.hbs.edu/databases/by_subject/credit_ratings.html). You'll notice that they are all fee-based and skew toward the high-end finance data side of things. Also, if a patron is looking for historical ratings from all three of the major ratings sources, this can be difficult because many of the sources carry only one or two ratings sources at most, and the length of their bond ratings back files can vary, too.

These are just a few things to keep in mind when faced with bond-related questions. Even after dealing with multiple requests like these over the years, they are still a challenge for me.

S&P's NetAdvantage Bond Reports
See page 19 (chapter 2, "The Business Reference Resource [aka the Business Reference Database]"). Standard & Poor's NetAdvantage database pulls together a number of their print publications, including Bond Reports that contain corporate bond data and ratings.

Mergent Bond Reports or BondViewer
www.mergent.com/productsServices-print-bondRecord.html
http://bv.mergent.com
Corporate bond ratings from Moody's, available in print or online. The Mergent BondViewer product can be included in the Mergent Online database as part of a company's Long Term Debt coverage. Moody's bond ratings as well as S&P and Fitch are part of BondViewer.

Fitch Ratings
www.fitchratings.com
As mentioned earlier, Fitch, along with S&P and Moody's, is one of the major bond rating agencies. With free registration, users can access quite a bit of corporate, municipal, and other bond data, although advanced screening capabilities and access to historical data requires a premium subscription.

InvestingInBonds.com
http://investinginbonds.com
This site from the Securities Industry and Financial Markets Association (SIFMA) is a good primer on bond research. For even more information, you can also check out SIFMA's main site www.sifma.org.

BondsOnline
www.bondsonline.com
This site covers U.S. corporate bonds, U.S. municipal bonds, U.S. Treasury and Federal Agency securities, bond funds, and convertible bonds.

TreasuryDirect
www.treasurydirect.gov
Treasury bonds and other investment products are available through the U.S. Treasury Department. This site has some basic information and more.

Yahoo! Bonds Center
http://bonds.yahoo.com
Yahoo! Bonds Center has some bond research information as well as some great explanations of all things bond related under their "Bonds Primer" section.

CNNMoney Bonds and Interest Rates (free)
http://money.cnn.com/data/bonds/
This is another option for getting quick bond data or some basic explanations of bonds and bond markets.

SOURCES OF MUTUAL FUND INFORMATION

Mutual funds are large pools of money managed by an investment company. For a basic overview of mutual funds, check out How Stuff Works: http://money .howstuffworks.com/question727.htm.

S&P's NetAdvantage Fund Reports
See page 19 (chapter 2, "The Business Reference Resource [aka the Business Reference Database]"). Standard & Poor's NetAdvantage pulls together a number of their print publications, including their Fund Reports.

Morningstar (some free content)
www.morningstar.com
See page 18 (chapter 2, "The Business Reference Resource [aka the Business Reference Database]"). Morningstar provides investment research on all kinds of investment offerings, but one of the areas they are known for is their mutual fund research. Their print publications are often available in a public library setting.

Yahoo! Mutual Fund Center (free)
http://finance.yahoo.com/funds
Information on particular funds, quick looks at best performers, and lots of links to overviews of mutual funds and how they work.

Value Line Mutual Fund Survey

See page 20 (chapter 2, "The Business Reference Resource [aka the Business Reference Database]"). Value Line's Mutual Fund Survey has rankings on more than 7,000 mutual funds, full reports including analyst commentaries for an additional 1,500 leading funds, and profile summary reports on more than 10,000 mutual funds.

Mutual Fund Observer

www.mutualfundobserver.com

This noncommercial site replaced Fund Alarm in May 2011. There are discussion boards and commentaries as well as free profiles of two to four funds every month.

ICI Mutual Funds Connection

www.ici.org

Published by the Investment Company Institute, this informative site enhances public understanding of the investment company industry and the policy issues that affect it, particularly those involving legislation and regulation, the U.S. economy, and retirement security. Click on the "Statistics and Research" link for much more info, including PDF versions of their Investment Company Fact Book, which contains sections on mutual funds.

SOURCES OF COMMODITIES AND FUTURES INFORMATION

Commodities and futures markets set prices now to sell an item—that is, commodities such as wheat or metals—at a later time. For a quick overview of how futures contracts work, check out Investopedia (www.investopedia.com/university/futures/futures2.asp). That site also provides a nice overview of commodities (www.investopedia.com/university/commodities/default.asp).

U.S. Commodity Futures Trading Commission

www.cftc.gov

The U.S. Commodity Futures Trading Commission (CFTC) is to commodities what the SEC is to stocks. According to their website, "The CFTC assures the economic utility of the futures markets by encouraging their competitiveness and efficiency, ensuring their integrity, protecting market participants against manipulation, abusive trading practices, and fraud, and ensuring the financial integrity of the clearing process." Their website has a lot of information on commodities markets, including a handy glossary.

CME Group

www.cmegroup.com

In early 2008, the Chicago Board of Trade and the Chicago Mercantile Exchange merged to become the CME Group. Now they also include the New York

Mercantile Exchange and the Commodity Exchange Inc. and are one of the largest commodities futures exchange organizations in the world.

HISTORICAL STOCKS AND BONDS

If you have ever gone to look for an old stock price and come up empty-handed and shaking your head, you are not alone. Sometimes the date isn't even that far in the past, yet you still can't seem to find any indication that the company in question even existed. Although it may seem like these kinds of questions are designed to drive you slowly mad, this section of the book will help you the next time you're faced with a historical stock question.

It's a common scenario: a patron will ask for stock price information on a company that, perhaps unbeknownst to you, has either gone bankrupt or merged with another company, or changed in some other fundamental way. You go to your tried-and-true stock price resources thinking that you've got the question readily handled. And then you double- and triple-check those tried-and-true stock price resources and wonder why you're not finding what you need.

Here's the problem: those tried-and-true sources of stock price information, especially many of the free online ones, will often pull a defunct company's information from their system if it no longer has an active ticker symbol. And going through bankruptcy or merging with another company or changing in some other fundamental way will often result in a change in or deletion of a company's stock symbol.

For example, AOL merged with Time Warner back in early 2001, and if you try to find a stock price for AOL after that date there won't be one, since AOL as such doesn't exist anymore. In many systems that collect stock price info (both free and fee-based), trying to look up an earlier stock price from when AOL *did* exist won't work, either, because defunct tickers are dropped entirely with no indication that they were ever there to begin with. That means the data on AOL from that time period is gone completely from that resource now. I know—helpful, right? Oh, and just to make things more confusing in this particular example, Time Warner eventually decided to spin AOL off as a separate company and it's now back, but only with stock data available back to 2009 when the spin-off occurred.

In another example, Kmart merged with Sears in March 2005 to form a new company called Sears Holding Corp. Now Kmart's old ticker, KM, has been dropped from many systems and Sears's old ticker, S, has already been taken by Sprint Nextel Corp (and, yes, Sprint Nextel is the result of a merger between Sprint and Nextel that took place about five months after Sears became Sears Holding).

So, if a company's stock price or other information seems to be especially difficult to track down, do some background checking and other sleuthing. Search for articles that might mention a company's merger or bankruptcy, or try the *Who Owns Whom* directory (aka the Corporate Affiliations database, noted in chapter 2) to start looking for some clues on the company's past and present situation. Even easier, check out the Wikipedia entry for the company or do some other basic Internet searching to give yourself some clues to work with. Turn to print stock report guides like the S&P *Daily Stock Price Record* (below) or the *Wall Street Journal* or another newspaper's stock pages on microfilm. Some company information databases will include inactive companies (this may depend on your subscription), or a profile of an active version of the company may provide some information on the company's history.

Sources for Historical Stock and Bond Information

Historical newspapers, such as the New York Times, the Wall Street Journal, Investor's Business Daily, or local titles

If you have access to microfilm versions of historical newspapers and the date you are looking for falls sometime before the mid-2000s, you may be able to access daily stock prices from the business section. Starting around 2006, many newspapers, including the *New York Times* and *Wall Street Journal*, stopped printing daily stock listings. What this holds for the future of historical stock price research, I don't know, but that's another story entirely.

Daily Stock Price Record from Standard & Poor's

Sometimes a resource like this will be your only option for finding historical stock prices. It doesn't cover every exchange, but it does give high, low, and closing prices for many companies going back to 1962.

Mergent (Moody's) manuals (print)

These can be useful if you don't need daily stock prices but are looking for a ballpark estimate.

Stocks, Bonds, Bills and Inflation (SBBI) Classic Yearbook from Ibbotson (now owned by Morningstar)

http://corporate.morningstar.com

This source gives rates of returns on the capital markets in the United States from 1926 to latest year. It includes returns for large and small company stocks, corporate and government bonds, and inflation.

CRB Commodity Yearbook (from the Commodity Research Bureau)

www.crbtrader.com/fund/

The Commodity Research Bureau (CRB) Commodity Yearbook provides information on more than one hundred domestic and international commodities. Find information on seasonal patterns and historical data from the past ten years as well as current pricing and trading patterns on a monthly and annual basis.

Investment Statistics Locator by Linda Holman Bentley and Jennifer J. Kiesl (Phoenix, AZ: Oryx Press, 1995)

Although it hasn't been updated in a while, this guide can come in handy if you need some clues for finding specific investment statistics such as daily stock prices, industrial averages, and treasury bill prices.

What to Do with an Old Stock Certificate

www.prattlibrary.org/locations/bst/index.aspx?id=3030&mark=stock

From the Enoch Pratt Free Library in Baltimore, Maryland, this page provides some handy starting points and tips for anyone trying to figure out whether an old stock certificate is worth anything.

Cashing In on Collectible Stock and Bond Certificates

www.bankrate.com/brm/news/investing/20011030a.asp

From Bankrate.com, this page provides some information on finding professional researchers to help you with determining the value of old stock certificates.

Capital Changes Reporter (print and online)

Each entry in Capital Changes Reporter contains a chronological history of the stock's changes in corporate capital structure, including name changes, mergers, spin-offs, bankruptcy filings, stock splits, and other information that may help determine an old stock's current worth. It is arranged alphabetically by company. References to name changes are noted, sometimes leading the researcher to a dead end such as a bankruptcy notice, and other times resulting in an entry in which the stock is traded under a different name. There is also a database available that contains even more information—usually you'll only find this at larger business schools.

Directory of Obsolete Securities (Financial Information Inc.) (Jersey City, N.J.: Financial Information, Inc., 1970– [annual])

This directory "contains a brief profile of banks and companies whose original identities have been lost as a result of . . . change in name, merger, acquisition, dissolution, reorganization, bankruptcy, chapter cancellation." As the title implies, if your company is listed in this directory, chances are that it is currently worthless, although in some cases it may have some remaining value. This book includes company information going back to 1926 through the most recent volume, which appears to have been published in 1997.

Sources for Historical Annual Reports

ProQuest Historical Annual Reports

www.proquest.com/en-US/catalogs/databases/detail/pq_hist_annual _repts.shtml

This is one of the few databases out there whose name gives some clear indication of its content—annual reports covering about eight hundred Fortune 500 companies, some going back to the mid to late 1800s. It can be a useful tool if you're looking for information on a now-defunct company or for historical information on a modern company that has been around for a while.

Annual Reports at Academic Business Libraries
www.lib.purdue.edu/abldars/
This index is the result of a collaboration of twelve academic business libraries who merged the lists of their respective collections of annual reports to shareholders into one database of approximately thirty-eight thousand companies. The index identifies which library owns what reports and what years are covered. There is also information on the lending policies of each institution. For an excellent overview of the project, see the BRASS Academic BRASS newsletter (www.ala .org/rusa/sections/brass/brasspubs/academicbrass/acadarchives/vol6no1/ acadbrassv6no1_1).

Columbia Historical Corporate Reports Online Collection
http://library.columbia.edu/indiv/business/corpreports.html
In addition to being indexed in the above-mentioned Annual Reports at Academic Business Libraries, Columbia University's collection of annual reports has been digitized, and you can access the files through this site. The collection focuses primarily on companies that operated in and around New York. The collection contains close to eight hundred companies, and some of the reports go back to the mid-1800s through the 1960s.

SOCIALLY RESPONSIBLE INVESTING

Socially responsible investing (SRI) is an area that is gaining increasing interest, so I mention it briefly and include a few resources here. Also referred to as *ethical investing* or *sustainable investing*, SRI is intertwined with the corporate social responsibility (CSR) landscape. Both topics focus on companies whose operations support the greater good of society while still maintaining profitability.

In addition to the resources listed below, since patrons may be approaching this subject from a number of different angles, don't overlook resources related to business ethics in general and to other topics such as corporate governance, sustainability, and "green" shopping.

Sources for Socially Responsible Investing Information

EBSCO's Sustainability Reference Center
www.ebscohost.com/corporate-research/sustainability-reference-center/
This new product from EBSCO focuses on publications related to topics such as corporate social responsibility and renewable energy.

Ethical Corporation
www.ethicalcorp.com
A publication with a focus on news related to ethical investing and corporate social responsibility.

Wharton Library's Socially Responsible Investing Guide
http://gethelp.library.upenn.edu/guides/business/SRI.html
A great roundup of resources related to this topic.

University of Pittsburgh Corporate Social Responsibility Guide
www.library.pitt.edu/guides/business/CorporateSocialResponsibility
.html
This site isn't specifically focused on socially responsible investing, but it points to some useful free resources on related CSR topics.

MSCI Environmental, Social and Governance (ESG) Indices
www.msci.com/products/indices/thematic/esg/
MSCI ESG indexes rate companies on various criteria related to their corporate social responsibility. Through databases like Global Socrates and iRatings, users can research the KLD 400, one of the original social investment benchmarks, as well as carbon emissions and human rights practices.

Social Funds
www.socialfunds.com/csr
News and company overviews related to sustainability and socially responsible investing.

Corporate Register
www.corporateregister.com
Collection of corporate responsibility reports and related reports.

GlobalEdge's Social Responsibility Guide
http://globaledge.msu.edu/resourcedesk/social-responsibility/
Michigan State University's GlobalEdge project's guide to websites related to social responsibility.

Global Sustainability Project Guide
http://webservices.itcs.umich.edu/mediawiki/KresgeLibrary/index.php/
Global_Sustainability_Project
This is a guide I helped put together for a project by the Erb Institute for Global Sustainability Enterprise. It points to a number of relevant databases and websites that might come in handy for this kind of research.

"Socially Responsible Investing," by T. J. Billitteri (CQ Researcher 18 [August 29, 2008]: 673–696)
Retrieved from http://library.cqpress.com/cqresearcher/
If your library has access to CQ Researcher, this is a nice overview of the topic.

A BRIEF STORY, TO end this chapter: When I was first working at the public library, a patron came up to me while I was at the reference desk. It was a little bit slow, so I indulged him and listened attentively as he began to speak to me (seemingly) very knowledgeably about a few stocks, explaining clearly why I should think seriously about investing in them. He paused at some point and said, "Do you want to know how I learned about all of this?" I said, "Sure," whereupon he slowly raised the teddy bear he'd been holding down at his side so that it was peering over the edge of the reference desk. "Benjamin told me," he said, nodding with satisfaction. It was right about then that someone came looking for him and pulled him away apologetically. The lesson to take away from this is that the investment advice street runs both ways. Use your own discretion when taking investment advice from anyone, even legitimate analysts and investment databases. It may all sound pretty convincing, and there won't always be an obvious "Benjamin" to stop and give you pause. Conversely, just as librarians are not tax or legal or medical professionals, we also are not investment advisors ourselves, but rather "referrers" to sources of investment information. It never hurts to emphasize this with your patrons. Besides, even with access to all the investment analysis in the world, there is still no way to predict the future of the markets and companies (hence, the reason we don't quit our day jobs to go make it big on Wall Street—nor do we tell anyone else to do so).

START MAKING SENSE!

■ Browse through some of the investor education sites and see what catches your eye or sparks your curiosity.

■ Take a look at the market data coverage on the *Wall Street Journal's* web page (click on "Markets" and then "Market Data") or in the business section of another major newspaper.

■ Pick a company or two and, using a resource or two mentioned in this chapter, check on their closing stock price from last week as well as a few years ago on your birthday. Compare it to another company or index average from the same time period.

■ Pick a public company you know has changed over time, whether through a merger (e.g., Kmart and Sears) or acquisition (e.g., Comcast and NBC Universal) or simply because it doesn't exist anymore (e.g., Enron), and see if you can find their stock price from before whenever these changes occurred.

■ In addition to looking for current and historical stock prices, take a look at a few companies from a socially responsible investing viewpoint.

■ Review your collection (print and online) to see what kinds of resources you might have that would help with historical stock prices. How far back do they go? Better yet, pick a company like Sears or AOL and see what you can find in terms of historical prices.

7

CONSUMER RESEARCH AND MARKETING/ ADVERTISING

MANY BUSINESS REFERENCE questions entail some sort of quest for insight into the minds— and spending habits—of consumers. Patrons will often want to find detailed consumer demographic information such as income, age, ethnicity, and beyond into product purchasing data, television and movie viewing habits, and more. Underneath these kinds of questions, patrons are often trying to determine what the "next big thing" will be so that they can either invent it, market it, or invest in it (and I like to tell patrons that if I knew what the next big thing was, I wouldn't be working in a library!). Questions relating to who buys how much of what and how much does Company X spend (and on what channels—TV, radio, etc.) to advertise product Y, or on specific marketing strategies for a particular product or target market start to cross into the realm of proprietary company data (i.e., data that a company will not release and does not want their competitors to know). Unfortunately, though, this does not stop patrons from wanting to know and frequently asking these kinds of questions. All-knowing crystal balls aside, this kind of information, as you may have guessed, isn't something that's generally readily available. In fact, public companies aren't required to report their advertising/marketing budgets, and they are definitely not required to turn over their customer data. However, with a little ingenuity and creativity combined with some demographic and marketing resources, you can sometimes come up with a fairly robust picture for the patron as long as he's willing to be flexible.

The term *demographics* is often used in relation to data involving a consumer market, and marketing data is often tied in with the demographics of consumers, so I've combined the coverage of the two topics here (even though each could stand on its own as well as warrant its own entire book) under the umbrella category of consumer research. Also, the term *marketing* is sometimes used interchangeably with *advertising*. While there is some overlap, advertising generally refers to the subset of marketing that focuses on actual ad campaigns using media like television, billboards, radio, and Internet (and beyond, these days). Marketing is much broader and includes advertising and product sales, in addition to the customers themselves and matching a company's products and services to their needs. We'll go into each of these areas a little bit in this chapter.

GETTING STARTED: CONSUMER RESEARCH

Maybe you've dealt with the patron who comes into the library and breezily asks you for the number of consumers who regularly purchase pizza brand X or toothpaste brand Y? They never stop at just that, do they? They also want that data broken out by a specific town or city neighborhood, as well as broken out by race, gender, income, and numerous other criteria (eye color, favorite Muppet, whether lefty or righty . . . you've heard this all before, haven't you?). Each facet of the question—the age, the product, the location—adds an additional layer of complexity. Depending on how granular patrons want their data to be, these kinds of requests can snowball into frenzied searches if you're not careful. Adding facets can make an already difficult question much harder, if not impossible, unless some of the criteria are loosened.

So, now you know the truth—it's not you who can't find this kind of information, it's the nature of this kind of question in general.

That said, rather than being an exercise in frustration, this kind of question can turn into an opportunity to partner with the patron. While the exact answer may never be found, as you become more comfortable with marketing and demographic questions and resources, you'll be able to guide patrons toward data and other resources that will serve their needs, if not exceed their expectations. As with all business reference questions, you'll want to take a deep breath and step back from the request at first to consider what the question really is. This is one business reference area in particular where the reference interview and thinking creatively can save the day.

It's worth reiterating that the more narrow or specific the patron gets, the harder it will be to track down data. So don't get caught up in the details too soon and limit yourself to only one age range or small geographic area, or even one product or brand. Is the patron looking for sales of a specific brand (and color) of cell phone? Purchased by single females earning over $100,000 annually? Sold at Walmarts in Montana? And how much Verizon spent on TV ads airing in Bozeman? Before you run away vowing never to make another phone call again, step back and break the question into its component parts. Start with the broader industry question first—what can you find out about cell phones? Or smartphones? Or mobile communications? (Remember to brainstorm on all the relevant keywords!) Some industry coverage may include information about consumers or sales by channel, so keep an eye out for clues, just as you would with an industry search. You may be able to find some demographic information on consumers in Montana that can be further broken out by gender, income, and city. And, just as you would with an industry search, ask yourself, "Who cares?," and identify relevant groups that might collect data on the consumers you are interested in.

This kind of question may not have an "exact" answer that you can find, but using logic and creativity, an acceptable approximation might be possible. Similar to how you would dive into a question on a small, fragmented industry, you will likely need to embark on a search for articles using keywords such as [*company name*], [*general product name*], *consumers or target market*, and similar strategies (e.g., *cell phones and consumers and demographics*; *Android and (women or females) and market*; or *mobile phones and Montana and consumers*). There is a lot out there in general news as well as in trade and industry publications covering consumers from all kinds of angles. The trick is to be creative in your searching and to not search for everything all at once, expecting to find a handy spreadsheet with all the data points laid out for you. And an often-overlooked category of resources for gaining insight into the minds of people (aka consumers) are the myriad social surveys, news, and marketing polls that are out there. Some of these are noted in their own section of the resource list below, along with additional websites as well as print resources.

A BRIEF WORD ABOUT MSAS AND DMAS

Often someone looking into a company or industry wants to know who the customers are. Or, conversely, they will want to pick a certain geographic area and learn about who lives there—age, income, education, and so on. In marketing, these geographic areas are often broken out into two areas:

The U.S. government divides the country into *metropolitan statistical areas*, or MSAs. Each MSA includes the metropolitan city and the surrounding suburban areas as defined by the U.S. government.

A *designated market area*, or DMA, is a geographical region set up by the Nielsen Company (of Nielsen ratings fame). The counties that make up a city's television viewing area define a DMA. DMAs are ranked in order by the number of households with televisions. All U.S. counties, except the North Slope of Alaska, fall into a DMA. DMA markets cover a larger area than MSA markets.

Some sources will break out data into both DMAs and MSAs, but others will only do one and many, neither. Being aware of the definitions can help you more accurately fulfill your patrons' requests.

For a great overview of MSAs, DMAs, and lots of other geographical designations, check out this page from a company called Marketing Systems Group: www .genesys-sampling.com/pages/Template2/site2/61/default.aspx.

RESOURCES: CONSUMER RESEARCH
Note: See also the relevant sections in chapter 2, "The Business Reference Resource (aka the Business Reference Database)."

New Strategist Publications Inc. (print series)
www.newstrategist.com
New Strategist publishes books that focus on various segments of U.S. consumers. These are great for getting quick snapshots of particular demographic groups or spending trends.

- American Generations series; for example, *Millennials: Americans Born 1977 to 1994*
- Who's Buying series; for example, *Who's Buying for Pets*
- Money series; for example, *Household Spending: Who Spends How Much on What* and *Best Customers: Demographics of Consumer Demand*
- Consumer series; for example, *American Marketplace: Demographics and Spending Patterns*

American FactFinder
http://factfinder2.census.gov
American FactFinder is the search interface for finding data from the U.S. Census in the form of maps, tables, and reports. There is a lot here, but with some practice and lots of digging, you can get useful data out of it, like population counts, housing data, and quick fact sheets on towns, counties, zip codes, or states.

American Demographics (journal, fee-based)
www.adage.com/section/american_demographics/195
American Demographics used to be a stand-alone journal but is now a part of *AdAge* magazine. *American Demographics* contains special reports on the buying habits of Americans and other consumer-related marketing issues.

National Retail Federation
www.nrf.com

The National Retail Federation (NRF) is a great example of using an industry association as a source of data on that industry. I've included it here in the consumer research chapter, though, because much of their data relates to consumer behavior and spending. There is a wealth of information on the NRF site—click on "Industry Information" to be pointed to reports and research on consumer trends (e.g., back-to-college spending or Father's Day spending) as well as retail industry reports. The NRF publishes *Stores* magazine, which has a special issue every year listing the top 250 retailers in the world, ranked by revenues. This report and more is available on the NRF site.

American Customer Satisfaction Index
www.theacsi.org

Produced by the University of Michigan's Ross Business School, the ACSI measures ten economic sectors, forty-one industries (including e-commerce and e-business), and more than two hundred companies and federal or local government agencies, scoring them based on criteria that measure customer satisfaction.

Sales and Marketing Management: Survey of Buying Power
(November special issue of journal, fee-based)
www.salesandmarketing.com

Sales and Marketing Management is one of the major trade journals for executives in the sales and marketing field. Each November, they have a special issue that contains retail sales figures and the latest population and buying power statistics for every U.S. metropolitan and media market. Some older issues are available on their site for free.

Sourcebook of ZIP Code Demographics (out of print)
http://store.esri.com/esri/

In addition to standard demographic data and population changes and projections, this resource provides data broken out by zip codes on total businesses, total employment, spending potential indexes, "dominant lifestyles," and other useful categories. Unfortunately, it ceased publication in 2009. See the Esri Business Analyst entry on page 21 (chapter 2, "The Business Reference Resource [aka the Business Reference Database]") for their updated content.

Demographics USA (out of print)

Demographics USA is a directory of consumer data that breaks out, either by zip code or county (there are two separate editions), data such as age, sex, and ethnicity. In addition, the directory includes calculations on EBI (estimated buying power) and BPI (buying power index), which essentially show marketers who has money to spend on nonessential items. Like the sourcebook listed above, this too appears to have ceased publication in 2009, but I've decided to include it because you may have it in your stacks, and it could have some use if you're looking for older data.

NPD Group
www.npd.com
The NPD Group bills themselves as the "global leader in sales and marketing information." Click on their "Industry Expertise" tab to see the various areas of retail they cover. This is a data source you'll often see referred to in specialty trade and industry journals—and often you can hit the jackpot by stumbling across some bit of data from their articles. You can even incorporate NPD into your search strategy by adding it to an article search; for example, *apparel and NPD.*

The Nielsen Company
www.nielsen.com/content/corporate/us/en.html
Nielsen bills itself as the "world's leading marketing information company." You may have heard of Nielsen families and television ratings, but there are also Nielsen families who track all their purchases with a scanner, which Nielsen then packages into marketing data. They do publish some excellent, free newsletters on consumer topics (www.nielsen.com/us/en/insights.html).

Note that it is unlikely that any library setting will have access to NPD or Nielsen products due to their prohibitive cost and the restrictive contracts they have with the companies they track. Still, it's good to be aware of resources like these, if only to be better able to understand what is and isn't available to the average information consumer.

SOCIAL SURVEYS AND RELATED NEWS AND MARKETING POLLS

Sites that publish surveys and polling data can be valuable sources of insight on consumers and their mind-sets. The following is a list of some of the more well-known groups that manage and publish the results of these surveys and polls. While many of the questions focus on political topics, with some creative extrapolation, you and your patron may manage to come up with quite a bit of useful consumer data, too, from these resources.

> Gallup: www.gallup.com
> General Social Survey: www.norc.uchicago.edu/GSS + Website/
> Harris Interactive Polls: www.harrisinteractive.com/Insights/Harris
>   Vault.aspx
> Pew Research Center: http://pewresearch.org
> PollingReport.com: http://pollingreport.com

Roper Center Public Opinion Archives: www.ropercenter.uconn.edu
Zogby International: www.zogby.com/news/

RESOURCES: MARKETING AND ADVERTISING

Advertising Age (print and online)
http://adage.com
There is a wealth of information related to all things advertising and marketing in *Ad Age*. From lists of top advertisers and their agencies, brands and advertisers, to white papers and special reports on the Super Bowl, this is a resource worth checking out. While the free registration doesn't give you full-text access to everything here, it's a handy way to look at the kinds of topics *Advertising Age* covers and get ideas (especially if you happen to have *Advertising Age* full text through a database).

Brands and Their Companies (print and online)
www.gale.cengage.com
Not sure who makes Nutella? You can look up the brand in the *Brands and Their Companies* and be pointed to Ferrero USA, and then look up Ferrero and see that they also make Ferrero Rocher and Tic Tacs, among other products. (Who knew?) Discontinued brands are also included. A handy reference volume. Note that this content is available online through the Business and Company Resource Center database (soon to be replaced by the Business Insights: Essential database) as well as Gale Directory Library.

Encyclopedia of Consumer Brands (print)
http://tinyurl.com/encyofconsumerbrands
Approximately 600 of the "most popular brands in America" are highlighted in this three-volume set, published in 1994. Volume 1 covers consumable products, volume 2 covers personal products, and volume 3 covers durable goods. Some entries are for individual products, such as Twinkies or Scotch Tape, while others are for brand names such as Pillsbury or Sony. Entries include brand history, current (as of 1994) status, current (as of 1994) brand logos or photos, and sources for additional information. There is a new edition in the works set to publish in 2013, from what I can tell from calls to the publisher, the St. James Press imprint of Gale Cengage Learning. Stay tuned.

Trendwatching.com and Springwise (free online)
www.trendwatching.com/trends/
www.springwise.com
Trendwatching.com and their new sister site Springwise offer free newsletters that highlight some of the many trends they have identified among consumers. Want to know more about Massclusivity or the Insperience trend? While they might not

have the skinny on *every* trend, these are good sites to check for ideas on what's going on in the world of consumer tastes.

START MAKING SENSE!

- Review your collection to see what kinds of consumer data might be hiding within some of the resources.
- Browse through one or two of the polling/survey sites to see how your opinions compare. Be on the lookout for potentially useful topics that you can turn to later when faced with a consumer-related question.
- Identify some local or regional groups that might provide census and other demographic information for your area in particular.
- Gather the resources you can find that are most relevant to your patron population and design a pathfinder or guide.

8

BUSINESS (AND OTHER) STATISTICS

B ECAUSE STATISTICAL DATA of all kinds often plays a role in a business reference question scenario, in this chapter I cover some of the key resources you'll want to know about. The word *statistics* is, by itself, a very vague and broad term, and adding *business* as a qualifier doesn't necessarily help narrow things down. Statistics can be found almost anywhere and, truth be told, you can find statistics in almost any of the databases or other resources noted throughout the book. In this chapter, the focus will be on resources that don't have a particular subject focus (e.g., finance or consumer demographics) but instead offer more general numerical data that may be of use to you in your hunt for business reference information. Statistics can encompass any number of topics, not just those that are business related, so it's especially important to keep some of the resources in this chapter in mind when dealing with business reference. These are resources that at first glance will not stand out to you as business reference resources, per se, and so will require a little more creativity in order to be fully exploited.

As is the case with industry data and consumer data, the more specific and narrow the statistic in question, the harder it will be to find. This is the case for most kinds of data queries, especially those that are business related. And when you're hunting for statistical data, the trick is not only to find what you need but also to find it broken out in exactly the right way—for example, finding monthly retail sales versus annual, dollars sales of iPods versus product units, income levels by zip code versus county. This can add another layer of complexity, so don't forget some of the strategies discussed in earlier chapters to keep yourself from spinning your wheels too much.

GETTING STARTED: BUSINESS (AND OTHER) STATISTICS

It's important to determine whether the patron needs just a quick number or a long run of consistent, comparable data. Try to ask some questions about what the numbers will be used for and what kind of range they need to cover.

Some things to keep in mind when dealing with statistical reference questions:

Just because a number is found does not make it a good or even correct number.

It's especially important to check sources when dealing with statistics. Look for sources of data and then work backward—there may be more available than published.

Just as with industry research, ask yourself, "Who cares?," and try to identify groups that would care about the numbers you're looking for.

Don't forget print sources when it comes to statistics—check those reference shelves.

A lot of statistical data, if it's packaged the way you want it and involves a comprehensive study, will cost money. Sorry.

RESOURCES FOR GENERAL BUSINESS AND OTHER STATISTICS
Note: See also the relevant sections in chapter 2, "The Business Reference Resource (aka the Business Reference Database)."

Government Information by Type of Business Need
www.anderson.ucla.edu/x14415.xml
This index from UCLA's Anderson School of Management Library is broken out by category and is a great pointer to all kinds of statistics from government sources.

Data.gov
www.data.gov
Data.gov is a portal to statistics and data sets produced by federal government agencies and offices. The intention is that it will eventually replace the FedStats site (http://fedstats.gov), which has been available since 1997 and allows users to access statistical data produced by the federal government without having to

know which agency produces which particular statistics. For now, FedStats may have some data that Data.gov doesn't yet, so it's best to be aware of both.

USA.gov (U.S. government websites portal)
www.usa.gov
USA.gov (formerly known as FirstGov) is intended to transcend the traditional boundaries of government to connect users to all U.S. government information and services. Launched in September 2000 and renamed in January 2007, USA .gov searches over 186 million pages of government information, services, and online transactions. USA.gov also provides a topical index and links to state and local government, as well as contacts with government officials. Another good place to start when you're not sure which agency or group tracks the info you're looking for.

Statistical Abstract of the United States
www.census.gov/compendia/statab/
October 1, 2011, was a sad day for business and other researchers everywhere. The U.S. Census Bureau, which has compiled the Statistical Abstract of the United States since 1878, officially announced that, due to budget cuts, it was terminating the collection of data for the Statistical Abstract (and some related, supplemental publications). A Facebook group called Save the US Statistical Abstract! (https://www.facebook.com/groups/193019537404038/) was formed, and although the 2012 edition will be the last to be compiled and published by the U.S. Census Bureau, it appears that the Statistical Abstract will, in fact, be saved! In March 2012 ProQuest announced that it would take over publication of this indispensable reference work beginning with the 2013 edition. You can access Statistical Abstracts going back to the first 1878 edition through the Census site for now. It remains to be seen what kind of access to the data ProQuest will provide. In terms of making the best use of the Statistical Abstracts, remember that the tables in it are excellent pointers to the original sources of data. As with the print version, you'll want to go to the index section first and find out which number chart you need (or you can browse by category).

OFFSTATS (for country statistics)
www.offstats.auckland.ac.nz
See page 94 (chapter 9, "International Business").

U.S. Census Bureau
www.census.gov
The U.S. government tracks a lot of statistics, and much of this statistical tracking and research is overseen by the Census Bureau. Their American FactFinder tool was mentioned in chapter 7, "Consumer Research and Marketing/Advertising," but there are many more statistics available. Their "Subjects A to Z" page (www

.census.gov/main/www/a2z) is an excellent way to browse through their offerings. You never know what you might find. There's a substantial business category, but beyond that you'll also see data related to construction, foreign trade, education, and more. Three big projects of the U.S. Census Bureau are highlighted below.

Economic Census
www.census.gov/econ/census/
The Economic Census, as you might guess, provides much of its data in statistical form. They've recently snazzed up their website and have some useful tutorials and ideas for how to use the data they provide. Use the Economic Census if you're looking for business counts, information on business owners, and related statistics. See page 49 (chapter 4, "Industry Research") for more on this site.

Statistics of U.S. Business
www.census.gov/csd/susb/
Statistics of U.S. Businesses (SUSB) is an annual series (although 2009 is the most current year available) that provides national and state-level data on numbers of businesses and employees, broken out by industry. The series excludes data on self-employed individuals, employees of private households, railroad employees, agricultural production employees, and most government employees.

County Business Patterns
www.census.gov/econ/cbp/
County Business Patterns is an annual series that provides county economic data by industry. Like Statistics of U.S. Businesses, County Business Patterns excludes data on self-employed individuals, employees of private households, railroad employees, agricultural production employees, and most government employees.

Business Statistics of the United States (print)
www.bernan.com
Includes historical data for nearly twenty-seven industries, spanning thirty years for annual data and four years for monthly. This is a useful addition to the reference shelf for pulling quick numbers rather than wrestling with the many online sources.

Liber8
http://liber8.stlouisfed.org
The Research Library of the Federal Reserve Bank of St. Louis, Liber8 serves as a portal of economic and banking info for librarians and students.

Frequently Used Sites Related to U.S. Federal Government Information
www.library.vanderbilt.edu/romans/fdtf/statistics.html
Sponsored by ALA's Government Documents Round Table (GODORT), this is a useful guide to top-level sources of statistics. There are links to general pages but also to specific topics such as agriculture, energy, housing, and even business.

ProQuest Statistical Insight (fee-based)

http://cisupa.proquest.com

In May 2011, ProQuest acquired the Statistical Insight product from LexisNexis. The interface allows you to search across numerous statistical sources, such as U.S. federal and state governments, universities, private associations and organizations, and independent research groups, as well as international and intergovernmental organizations.

World Almanac and Book of Facts

www.worldalmanac.com

Don't overlook the possibilities held within the pages (or in the online data files) of this tried-and-true reference tome. You can find lists of leading businesses by year, data on real estate debt by farm businesses, and a lot more. And, perhaps more importantly, as with tables from the Census and Statistical Abstract, you can check for the original source of the data to see if further clues are provided (if you, in fact, still need more data).

START MAKING SENSE!

- Browse through a print copy of the Statistical Abstract and/or the web version to see what you can find.
- Look up your hometown or a favorite U.S. city in the American FactFinder and see what kind of information comes up.
- Pick an industry and find out how many businesses are in operation using the Economic Census.

9

INTERNATIONAL BUSINESS

R EGARDLESS OF WHICH Core Four category you're dealing with (see page 5), many business reference questions also have an international facet. Whether someone is looking for a foreign company, determining a global market size, or examining the widget industry in Spain, you'll want to be prepared. International business research is a topic unto itself and an entire book could be devoted to it. (In fact, at least one has been devoted to the topic: *Going Global: An Information Sourcebook for Small and Medium-Sized Businesses* by Susan Awe is highlighted below). In this chapter, I list resources that focus on international data. Most provide at least some top-level country data and other information that should come in handy when a business reference question goes global on you.

GETTING STARTED: INTERNATIONAL BUSINESS

Often some of the "regular" business reference resources you're used to using include some range of international coverage, so don't overlook those. This coverage may be included automatically or may be available for an additional fee, depending on the resource. Many of the resources below cover a wide range of countries, but keep in mind that there are resources that specialize in specific countries or regional areas as well. Also, many resources that you may be familiar with because of their coverage of geographic or economic information (like World Book encyclopedia entries or other types of country guides) may come in handy in a business reference situation. So try not to get hung up on the business part of the equation and unwittingly rule out those kinds of resources.

As you expand the scope of your search to include sources published in the United Kingdom or other countries, be aware of spelling variations (*globalization* vs. *globalisation*), terminology (*diapers* vs. *nappies* and *consumer packaged goods* vs. *fast moving goods*), and transliteration issues (*Yeltsin* vs. *Jeltsin*). Legal and regulatory systems as well as industry classifications will differ country by country, so keep this in mind and take note of these differences as you find them, or alter your search strategies accordingly. Be aware of potential differences in cultures or protocols. There are etiquette books that cover business practices in particular, but even a general guide on local customs might be worth looking into, depending on the situation. Even differences in time zones can impact your search for international business information. If you've ever tried to call a business in Europe during the last two weeks of August, in India during Diwali, or in the U.K. at 3 p.m. EST, you'll know why being aware of holidays and time differences matter. Globalization and the Internet are changing some of this, but it is still something to keep in mind. Finally, this may seem like an obvious factor, but always make sure what currency a company's financials are being reported in. Depending on the source of the information, sometimes you can change the currency on the fly, but you don't want to have to retrace your steps later to confirm whether you noted down euros or yen or dollars.

International Company Filings

Most countries have agencies similar to the SEC in the United States that oversee company registrations in some way, but availability of the filings will vary greatly. The U.K.'s Companies House has a site that lists worldwide registries (scroll down: www.companieshouse.gov.uk/links/introduction.shtml). Also, for Canadian companies, the Sedar site (www.sedar.com/homepage_en.html) is useful. An Official Company Registrars page (www.rba.co.uk/sources/registers.htm) provides a little more background on that topic as well as some additional resources for international business research.

RESOURCES: INTERNATIONAL BUSINESS

Note: See also the relevant sections in chapter 2, "The Business Reference Resource (aka the Business Reference Database)."

NationMaster

www.nationmaster.com

This site is one of my favorite resources for international research. While you have to put up with some ads, this is a great tool for country comparisons across a huge range of topics, including crime statistics, agriculture, disasters, and democracy. As they say on their website, "We want to be the web's one-stop resource for country statistics on everything from soldiers to wall plug voltages." Aggregating data from sources like the CIA World Fact Book, the United Nations, and the Organisation for Economic Co-operation and Development (see below), this is a great tool to use for working backward to see who tracks the data you're looking for. (Note: A statemaster.com counterpart is also available for U.S. states.)

BRASS's "Best of the Best" Business Websites—
International Business

www.ala.org/rusa/sections/brass/brassprotools/
bestofthebestbus/bestbestbusiness

This is a great list of free, online resources for international business information. Some are duplicated on this list, but others are not.

GlobalEdge

http://globaledge.msu.edu

GlobalEdge is a comprehensive starting point for global research from Michigan State University's Center for International Business Education and Research (CIBER). It's essentially a meta site with access to international business and trade information, as well as economic trends and an index to information resources.

World Bank Data, including World Development Indicators

http://data.worldbank.org

See page 26 (chapter 2, "The Business Reference Resource [aka the Business Reference Database]"). Formerly a fee-based product, the World Bank recently opened up their data sets, including World Development Indicators (WDI). WDI provides annual cultural, demographic, economic, environmental, and health data for 210 countries since 1960. Other data sets available through the World Bank include Africa development indicators, global development finance, and the global economic monitor.

UNData
http://data.un.org
This is an award-winning site that pulls together the numerous statistical databases maintained by the United Nations. Browse by country or topic or even peruse popular searches. It's easy to search keywords across the data. A glossary is provided, as well as a detailed description of each of the data sets (thirty-two at last count).

OFFSTATS
www.offstats.auckland.ac.nz
OFFSTATS is a great directory of free country statistics from official sources, culled from all over the Internet and the world. Searchable by country, region, or topic.

Business without Borders
www.businesswithoutborders.com
Business without Borders (BwB) covers various industries and topics for U.S. businesses that are looking to expand internationally. Produced by HSBC Bank, BwB pulls together a number of resources, including "Doing Business In . . .," country guides, and much more.

Population Reference Bureau
www.prb.org/DataFinder.aspx
The Population Reference Bureau is a research organization focused on data related to population, health, and the environment. Their Datafinder tool covers the United States using data from the census and covers international regions and countries by pulling together data from their own research as well as organizations like the United Nations and the International Energy Agency. Worth a look to see what kind of information is available for whatever area of the world you are researching.

Fortune Global 500
http://money.cnn.com/magazines/fortune/global500/
The Global 500 is the international version of Fortune's standard "500" list, which focuses only on America's largest corporations. This is a handy site for identifying large global companies and the countries they are headquartered in.

U.S. International Trade Commission for Import Data
http://dataweb.usitc.gov
The ITC's dataweb section offers online access to lots of import and export data, which often comes up during an international business reference situation. It's not the easiest site in the world to search, but if you can manage to get to their USITC Tariff Database, you can try to identify the code for your product and get import information going back a number of years.

Trade Stats Express for Export and Import Data
http://tse.export.gov
Trade Stats Express is a handy website for quick, top-level import and export data, and while it doesn't get as specific as you might want, it's a little more straightforward than some international trade data search systems. For a brief explanation of the import and export code system (the Harmonized Tariff System), see www.census.gov/foreign-trade/faq/sb/sb0008.html.

Internet Public Library Newspapers
www.ipl.org/div/news/
A quick way to identify local papers in various countries that may come in handy later on in your search.

Organisation for Economic Co-operation and Development (OECD) (some free)
www.oecd.org
The Organisation for Economic Co-operation and Development is a big source of global macroeconomic and trade data. Some reports and data are available for free. Click on the "Statistics" link on their main page to see a list of all the categories of statistics they cover, or drill down by country. SourceOECD, their fee-based product, is mentioned in chapter 2.

International Monetary Fund (some free)
www.imf.org
The International Monetary Fund (IMF) is another respected source for global financial and economic data.

World Bank e-Library
http://elibrary.worldbank.org
The World Bank e-Library is a subscription-based portal to full-text books, reports, journals, working papers, and other formal documents from the World Bank. These are especially useful for research into developing countries.

Print Resources for International Business Research

Going Global: An Information Sourcebook for Small and Medium-Sized Businesses by Susan C. Awe (Santa Barbara, CA: Libraries Unlimited, 2009)
www.abc-clio.com/product.aspx?isbn=9781591586517
This book targets small and medium-sized business owners and provides tips and resources for setting up an international business as well as using the Internet to expand sales globally.

Europa World Year Book
www.europaworld.com/pub/about#details.ewyb
The *Europa World Year Book* is a fairly standard reference source and is found on most academic and public library reference shelves. The two-volume annual set provides detailed country profiles and analytical, statistical, and directory data for over 250 countries and territories. An online version is now available as well.

Encyclopedia of Global Industries
www.gale.cengage.com
This encyclopedia from Gale Cengage Learning looks at 125-plus business sectors of global significance and discusses "the origins, development, trends, key statistics, and current international character." Some of the industries included are aircraft, biotechnology, computers, Internet services, motor vehicles, pharmaceuticals, semiconductors, software, and telecommunications.

International Yearbook of Industrial Statistics
www.unido.org/doc/3544
Now published by Edward Elgar, the *International Yearbook of Industrial Statistics* breaks out by manufacturing subsector and by country comparative statistics on performance and trends in manufacturing. Data is compiled by the United Nations Industrial Development Organization (UNIDO).

Industrial Commodity Statistics Yearbook
http://millenniumindicators.un.org/unsd/industry/icsy_intro.asp
This is another good source of comparative data from the United Nations, this time focusing on world production of various commodities. The *Yearbook* provides statistics on the production, in physical quantities, of about 530 industrial commodities by country, geographical region, economic grouping, and for the world in 590 tables. It includes data for a ten-year period for about two hundred countries. These kinds of global statistical sources can take time to compile, which is why the 2008 edition is currently the most recent available, although access to more recent statistics can be purchased through the Industrial Commodity Statistics Database.

Nations of the World: A Political, Economic and Business Handbook
www.greyhouse.com/nations.html
This contains handy economic and business information for more than two hundred countries, including travel- and tourism-related states.

World Business Directory
Published by Gale Cengage, the *World Business Directory* has directory information on over 130,000 companies active in international trade. The companies are arranged by 180 countries, giving address, telephone/fax, officers, sales, number of employees, and activities or products. The index (volume 4) provides cross-

referencing by product, industry, and company name. It is an excellent source of competitors, prospective employers, trading partners, and joint venture opportunities. (It appears that this is no longer in print, but the content may be available as part of the Gale Virtual Reference Collection database.)

International Financial Statistics Locator by Dominica M. Barbuto (New York: Garland, 1995)

Although it's a little bit dated at this point (last published in 1995), the *International Financial Statistics Locator* might help you out in a bind if you need to know who tracks certain international financial data. Don't throw this out yet if you have it in your stacks.

COUNTRY GUIDES

Harvard Business School Baker Library Country and International Guide

www.library.hbs.edu/guides/international.html

This site is a great pointer to sources of international business information. Some of the sources listed here are noted, as well as additional free online sources and some sources available through Harvard only.

Intersource Country Insights from the Centre for Intercultural Learning (free online)

www.intercultures.ca/cil-cai/countryinsights-apercuspays-eng.asp

Issues covered for each country include communication styles, displays of emotion, dress, punctuality, formality, stereotypes, preferred managerial qualities, and conflict in the workplace. Produced by the Canadian government.

CIA World Factbook

https://www.cia.gov/library/publications/the-world-factbook/

The *CIA World Factbook* is widely used. Country profiles include information on geography and communication networks and transportation in addition to the traditional economic and demographic data snapshots. The University of Missouri–St. Louis has a historical (1990–2008) set of the *CIA World Factbook* (www.umsl.edu/services/govdocs/alpha_list.html).

Articles from the Economist

www.economist.com/topics/

You can use this page to point you toward articles in the *Economist* on your country or international city of choice. The *Economist* used to make some of their Country Briefings data, including forecasts, available on their website, but they now point visitors to their Economist Intelligence Unit product (mentioned in chapter 2).

Country Analysis Briefs from the Energy Information Administration
www.eia.gov/countries/
These profiles come from the Energy Information Administration (EIA), a division of the Department of Energy focused on gathering statistics. Information on oil, gas, and other energy issues by country and by international region is highlighted.

State Department's Country Background Notes
www.state.gov/r/pa/ei/bgn/
Country profiles here give a brief snapshot of a country's people, history, government, economics, and politics, with additional focus on military and foreign relations.

Export.gov's Country and Industry Market Reports (requires registration)
http://export.gov/mrktresearch/
From Export.gov, the United States government's portal to exporting and trade services, this site provides some market reports on a number of industries in various countries and also includes information on exporting in general and other trade issues.

International Monetary Fund (IMF) Country Information
www.imf.org/external/country/
Reports on IMF-member countries, focusing primarily on economic issues and country risk.

Culturegrams (fee-based)
www.culturegrams.com
Available in a country-by-country print edition as well as in an online database format, Culturegrams provides a nice snapshot of a country's economic and cultural landscape. Brief profiles of customs, diet, religion, and other lifestyle issues are covered.

AND DON'T FORGET:

- Country home pages (yes, they exist!) and tourist bureaus
- The regional versions of various search engines (Google UK or Google Japan), Hoover's, and other international search engines such as www.searchenginecolossus.com.

OTHER USEFUL INTERNATIONAL BUSINESS RESOURCES

Directory of Online Dictionaries and Translators
www.word2word.com/dictionary.html

BabelFish
http://babelfish.yahoo.com

Google Translate
http://translate.google.com

START MAKING SENSE!

- Take a look at your collection (online and print) to familiarize yourself with some of the international business resources you may have.
- If you've got an international data quest on your hands, start with some of the resources mentioned here, check to see what data sources they were using, and follow those leads.
- Pick one or two countries and see what kind of information you can find out about them in some of the resources above.

10

SMALL BUSINESS

IN ANY BUSINESS reference setting you can expect to encounter requests for information from people who want to start a small business. In addition to the resources discussed throughout this book, a few others are geared specifically toward the small business entrepreneur or focused on data about small businesses. These resources will be especially useful in a public library setting that serves small business patrons, as well as in academic settings that may deal with questions involving entrepreneurship.

GETTING STARTED: SMALL BUSINESS

Small business patrons will likely need resources beyond the scope of the company and industry research assistance you can provide at the library. They may have questions about financing their business; local, state, and federal tax questions; registration requirements; and other related legal issues. That said, many of the resources described below will at least get them pointed in the right direction. Not to mention that, with the help of this book, you can also get them started on their industry and consumer research as well!

RESOURCES: SMALL BUSINESS

Small Business Administration
www.sba.gov
The Small Business Administration (SBA) website is a great resource to point people toward. In addition to business plan templates and information on financing and grants, there are also links to individual state sites and other useful sources.

SCORE, "Counselor to America's Small Business"
www.score.org
A resource partner of the SBA, SCORE offices are located throughout each state—and can help a small business by answering tax questions, helping find funding, and a lot more.

New York Public Library Small Business Resource Center
http://www.nypl.org/smallbiz
This is an excellent example (and source of) small business information. It also has great for ideas on enhancing your own library's services to small business.

Small Business Resource Center (Gale Cengage Learning) (fee-based)
www.gale.cengage.com
This database is an all-in-one resource that focuses on publications that target the needs of small business researchers. Included are electronic versions of the *Business Plans Handbook*, the *Encyclopedia of Business Information Sources*, *Encyclopedia of Management*, and *Small Business Management: A Framework for Success*. The Small Business Resource Center also features as dozens of titles from John Wiley and Sons, best known for the popular and easy-to-understand Dummies series, such as *Portable MBA Strategy*, 2nd ed.; *The 7 Irrefutable Rules of Small Business Growth*; and *Portable MBA in Entrepreneurship*.

Business Plans and Profiles Index
www.carnegielibrary.org/subject/business/bplansindex.html
From the Carnegie Library of Pittsburgh, this is a handy online index to two of the main print reference sources for business plans, the *Business Plans Handbook* and *Small Business Profiles*, plus pointers to individual titles on starting various kinds of businesses and links to online plans.

Biz Info Library
www.bizinfolibrary.org
This site is a collaboration between the Ewing Marion Kauffman Foundation, the Edward Lowe Foundation, and the James J. Hill Reference Library and provides some great information on starting and growing a business. Categories covered include legal and tax considerations, exit strategies, customer service, and strategic planning, among others.

Business Plans Handbook
www.referenceforbusiness.com/business-plans/
From Gale Cengage Learning, a handy multivolume collection of sample business plans, indexed by type of business. The Carnegie Index listed above also indexes the Business Plans Handbook and points to the print volumes as well some links to online versions. The Business Plans Handbook is also available through a number of Gale databases, such as their Small Business Resource Center and their Virtual Reference Library. This site provides free access to most of the Business Plans Handbook content.

Encyclopedia of Small Business
www.referenceforbusiness.com/small/
Also from Gale Cengage Learning, this encyclopedia defines and then details issues faced by small businesses, including accounting, competitive bids, and outsourcing, among many other topics. Also available through Gale's Small Business Resource Center and their Virtual Reference Library. This site provides free access to most of the Encyclopedia of Small Business content.

Going Global: An Information Sourcebook for Small and Medium-Sized Businesses by Susan C. Awe (Santa Barbara, CA: Libraries Unlimited, 2009)
www.abc-clio.com/product.aspx?isbn=9781591586517
See also page 95 (chapter 9, "International Business"). This book has some really practical information for small businesses that, like it or not, will have to consider the global marketplace at some point.

BizMiner
www.bizminer.com
BizMiner is a great resource for finding local industry financial and market analysis down to a zip code level, failure rates of businesses, and more. Owned by the Brandow Company, some of their industry ratio data is made available freely online through their BizStats site, mentioned in chapter 5, Company Finance.

Catalog of Federal Domestic Assistance
www.cfda.gov
There are currently fifteen types of federal assistance available to search, including surplus equipment, training, guaranteed loans, and grants. The Catalog of Federal Domestic Assistance (CFDA) database covers all federal programs available to state and local governments (including the District of Columbia); federally recognized Indian tribal governments; territories (and possessions) of the United States; domestic public, quasi-public, and private profit and nonprofit organizations and institutions; specialized groups; and individuals. In some cases, there may be some programs or funding available for small businesses, but it's not the case that there

is "free money" out there for wanna be entrepreneurs, no matter what the late night infomercials are telling them.

Harvard Business School's Baker Library Subject Guides: Venture Capital and Private Equity (free online)
www.library.hbs.edu/guides/venture/
This industry guide from Harvard Business School's Baker Library is useful for identifying sources of information on venture capital sources. Make sure to look to the left of the screen for additional content broken out by format, including trade journals associations.

Financial Studies of the Small Business (Financial Research Associates) (print)
It appears that this title is no longer in print as of 2007 or so, but if you have a copy in your reference stacks, it could still provide some useful information. This source provides industry ratios on small business. Using as criteria total capital-ization under $2 million, financial statements for over 30,000 firms, provided by 1,500 independent certified public accounting firms, geographically dispersed throughout the country. (Additional industry ratios resources are covered in chapter 4, "Industry Research.")

Small Business and the Public Library: Strategies for a Successful Partnership by Luise Weiss, Sophia Serlis-McPhillips, and Elizabeth Malafi (Chicago: American Library Association, 2011)
www.alastore.ala.org/detail.aspx?ID=2648
This title (from the publisher of *Making Sense of Business Reference*) provides some great ideas for outreach to small business patrons and highlights how libraries can stay relevant by addressing the needs of the small business community.

START MAKING SENSE!

- Take a look at your collection (online and print) to familiarize yourself with some of the small business resources you may have.
- Many libraries are offering tailored services to their small busi-ness and entrepreneurial patrons—is your library already doing this? If not, take a look at sites like the NYPL Small Business Resource Center and see what you might be able to incorporate into your own library's services.
- Follow up on some of the resources mentioned in the Social Me-dia Resources section in Chapter 3, Company Information, and see what takes shape.
- Identify your local SBA and SCORE offices and other nearby re-sources for small businesses. Check out what projects they have going on or what resources they point to.

■ Consider partnering with local and regional organizations that offer small business support or that focus on economic development within your community. Take a look online by searching for your state's or county's name and terms such as *small business, startup, entrepreneurs*, or *economic development*. If nothing else, you can refer your patrons to their services, but many libraries are going even further and collaborating with groups like these to offer expanded services and resources. Here's an example from Michigan: www.gvsu.edu/misbtdc/region12/.

11

OTHER HANDY BUSINESS REFERENCE RESOURCES AND TIPS

S OME OF THE most important business reference resources don't fall easily into categories. This chapter emphasizes some useful search tools available through the open Internet. It will also highlight a number of people out there who can provide invaluable information and support in your quest to become a business reference champion. Finally, this chapter also reviews some resources and strategies for building a strong business reference collection. Combine these search skills and people resources with a solid, well-maintained collection of business reference resources and you're ready to take on the business reference world!

PEOPLE AND LIBRARY RESOURCES

Yes, there are real, live people out there who, whether individually or in groups, are working tirelessly in this battle to make sense of business reference. Turn to them for help and inspiration as well as to build your network of business reference buddies. And don't forget business school library sites and other library sites. These are great resources for getting ideas on how to present and organize your own library's business information resources.

BusLib (e-mail group)

http://lists.nau.edu/cgi-bin/wa?A0=BUSLIB-L

I can't tell you how many times a BusLib member has saved me hours of searching. Sign up for the BusLib digest and see the kinds of questions that are asked (and answered!) by other helpful business librarians. Once you've signed up, you can also search the archives for helpful pointers. BusLib is great for business stumpers; if nothing else, you can run your question by this hearty group of business research experts to do a quick sanity check and see if you're on the right track or if you've overlooked something.

BRASS: Business Reference and Services Section of ALA's RUSA Division

www.ala.org/rusa/sections/brass

The BRASS site has a number of helpful links not only to the "Best of the Best Business Websites" and "Core Competencies for Business Reference," but also to handouts and presentations from the BRASS Program held each year at the ALA Annual Conference and more. Check it out! If you're not already, you may want to consider becoming a member of BRASS to fully leverage the opportunities to network with a great group of business reference librarians from both public and academic library settings. Full disclosure: I am a past chair of this section, and I consider BRASS my ALA home.

SLA Business and Finance Division

www.sla.org/content/community/units/divs/

http://bf.sla.org

The Business and Finance Division of the Special Libraries Association is an active and supportive group. You can join and sign up for their e-mails. Local chapters of the SLA, such as the Michigan Chapter (http://michigan.sla.org), may also have many members interested in business- and finance-related topics. SLA also has an Advertising and Marketing division as well as a Competitive Intelligence division, which might be of interest. SLA and any of its divisions are a great addition to your business reference support group network.

Harvard Business School's Baker Library

www.library.hbs.edu

Besides some great business guides and other tips, one feature I use on this site is the "new books in Baker Library." Click on "Books" to get to this link and see what they're collecting.

Lippincott Library at Wharton

www.library.upenn.edu/lippincott/

Check out their Business Database Wizard for some great ideas and also use their business FAQ to see if they can help you answer your own question.

Library of Congress: Business Reference Service

www.loc.gov/rr/business/

This is a useful resource on researching business and economics from the LOC. Although some of the pages haven't been updated in a while, there are some useful bibliographies and guides.

ipl2

http://ipl2.org/

In late 2009, the Librarians' Index to the Internet and the Internet Public Library merged to become the ipl2. When you've got that kind of librarian power maintaining and updating the site, it truly is "information you can trust." Business is only one of the many topics covered.

Bizlink from the Charlotte Mecklenburg Library

www.bizlink.org

A great business reference site from a public library. A good place to turn to when you're tired of being pointed to fee-based resources that you don't subscribe to.

Business Blog from Ohio University

www.library.ohiou.edu/subjects/businessblog/

Billed as "Tips, Tricks, and Tools for the Business Researcher," there is plenty to learn from this site. Great tutorial videos and subject guides are just a few of the things you'll find here posted by Chad Boeninger, Ohio University's Business Librarian.

Business Library 2.0 from the University of Florida

http://businesslibrary.uflib.ufl.edu/

This is an impressive collection of guides and other useful resources. You can also sign up for updates whenever a guide you're interested in has anything added to it. Also great for getting ideas for guides for your own library!

Jim Vileta's Business Research Launchpad

www.d.umn.edu/~jvileta/

This site hides a surprising amount of really helpful information related to all aspects of business research.

Citing Business Databases in APA Style

http://libguides.lib.msu.edu/citingbusdatabases

This page from Michigan State University can be very handy when you're trying to figure out how to cite what you just found in one of the databases discussed in this book. This is just one of many . . . if you do a Google search for citing business databases, you'll be directed to additional sources. Many give the citation format in APA style, although the Harvard Business School (HBS) Citation Guide (www.library.hbs.edu/guides/citationguide.pdf) is based on the *Chicago Manual of Style* method.

BizRefDesk—Land of the Free and the Good
www.bizrefdesk.blogspot.com

Terese Terry, a librarian at Wharton's Lippincott Library, is behind this blog, which is a great resource for keeping up on all kinds of handy new resources (as well as oldies but goodies).

ResourceShelf
www.resourceshelf.com

ResourceShelf's ResourceBlog will help keep you apprised of what's going on related to the world of online searching. Part of the FreePint family, a "global community for info pros," its companion sites, DocuTicker and FUMSI, are worth checking out, as well. DocuTicker highlights abstracts from the "gray literature" of think tanks, NGOs, research institutes, and other groups, and FUMSI (helping you Find, Use, Manage, and Share Information) has a number of free articles discussing hot topics related to business research.

INFOdocket and Full Text Reports
http://infodocket.com
http://fulltextreports.com

These sister sites are the newest brainchildren of Gary Price and Shirl Kennedy (who originally founded ResourceShelf and DocuTicker). They take care to note that INFOdocket is not ResourceShelf and Full Text Reports is not DocuTicker. Regardless, these sites are also useful resources for news about the information industry (INFOdocket) and for keeping up on new reports from trade associations, academe, research institutes, and more (Full Text Reports).

Bates Information Services
www.batesinfo.com

Another site to help you save time along your way to becoming a super searcher. Mary Ellen Bates is an independent researcher who has a lot of great ideas for sifting through piles of business haystacks. Check out her Librarian of Fortune blog and her Newsletter Archives under the Writing category to start. She also has a new writing outlet, MEB Adds Value (www.mebaddsvalue.com), which can help you take your business research findings to the next level.

MarcyPhelps.com
www.marcyphelps.com

Marcy Phelps is a contributor to FUMSI and the founder of Phelps Research. Her blog focuses on "tools and techniques for understanding and adding value to the information you find." It's regularly added to and worth a look.

SEARCH RESOURCES

Google
www.google.com

You may be looking at this entry and saying, "Well, duh . . . of course, I've heard of Google." I'm including it in this section in order to remind you to explore beyond the basic Google search and take advantage of some of their advanced search features (like limiting to certain domains like .org or finding sites that link to a site you're interested in). And see what you can find using some of their other search products, like Google Scholar or Google Books. Other Google tools that could be useful in a business reference setting are Google Insights for Search (www.google.com/insights/search/), Google Trends (www.google.com/trends/), and even Google Maps (http://maps.google.com).

Ask.com
www.ask.com

The previous entry notwithstanding, don't limit yourself to just one search engine. I heart Google and couldn't live without it, but just as with any committed relationship, it's not good to spend time only with each other. Try Ask.com (formerly Ask Jeeves) and check out the handy recommended search narrowers, results clustering, and other features. You may even turn up new information, as no single search engine (even Google) crawls everything. (If you remember a search engine called Teoma, that's now owned by Ask.com.)

The Wayback Machine
www.archive.org

While on the surface this website seems to have nothing to do with business reference, I have found it has come in handy on numerous occasions when trying to get a glimpse of what a company's website once looked like. The Internet Archive's Wayback Machine will show you links from past "snapshots" of how various URL's once looked (try a search for www.enron.com). An example of a site you can use to "think creatively" when doing business reference.

ResearchBuzz
Researchbuzz.me

ResearchBuzz's tagline, "Covering search engines, databases, and other online information collections since 1996," gives you a good sense of what they do. For new Google tricks, updates on various databases, some business-related, and more, ResearchBuzz is a useful and frequently-updated resource to know about.

Search Engine Watch
http://searchenginewatch.com

Let's face it, as librarians today we spend a lot of time searching the Web using search engines. Keep up on these tools of the trade here, and find out everything from search tips to search engine ratings to search engine news.

Technorati
http://technorati.com

The blogosphere is growing exponentially and is yet another area of the Web where we can find business information. Technorati searches blogs, plus keeps you up to date on blog-related news. (Keep in mind that Google now owns Blogger and also offers a "Blog Search" feature.)

COLLECTION DEVELOPMENT FOR BUSINESS REFERENCE

Some of you may be reading this book to help you develop your institution's business reference collection. And even if collection development isn't one of your primary duties, after reading this book you may be inspired to work with your collection development team to strategize how to build and grow your business collection. This section will present a few resources that may be of use. And don't forget that the materials pointed to throughout this book—including chapter 2, "The Business Reference Resource (aka the Business Reference Database)"— can serve as a sort of handy checklist to see what you do and don't have in your collection (keeping in mind the particular needs of your own patron base, of course).

Here are a few questions to consider when you're trying to build your institution's business collections:

Does your institution have an existing collection development policy?

- Have you read it?
- Does it need updating?
- What does it say, if anything, regarding your business collection?
- What does it say, if anything, regarding your print collection versus your electronic database and journal collection?

Who is ultimately responsible for your business collection?

- Do subject specialists partner with collection development specialists?

When dealing with online/electronic products, have you considered access issues?

- Is there a cap on the number of users and/or are simultaneous users allowed?
- Who owns the content? In other words, do the archives disappear if you don't renew?
- Is remote access enabled, or do users need to be on-site to use them?

What do you already own?

- Have you checked for overlapping titles or content in your article and other databases?
- Have you looked for online resources that are freely available and considered how to integrate them into your collection?

Have you looked into consortium pricing options?

- Do you know what consortiums your library belongs to?

Has your library considered the marketing and outreach opportunities that a strong business collection might provide?

Have you thought about how you can solicit input from your patrons and involve them in the collection development process?

In academic libraries, have you looked into the major assignments that will be supported by your business collection? (This can provide a good excuse—not that you need one—to reach out to faculty.)

In public libraries, have you developed a relationship with your local small business community? (For example, some libraries offer a "corporate card" for a small fee that allows businesses to remotely access library databases. These subscriptions can be tricky to negotiate with vendors, but potentially worth it for the PR you could generate.)

Finally, once you've built it, have you considered how you'll promote your fabulous business reference collection?

- How will you gauge success?
- How will you maintain the collection, not only financially, but also practically—staying current on new features and/ or products?

Resources: Collection Development for Business Reference

Selected Core Resources for Business Reference

www.ala.org/rusa/sections/brass/brassprotools/corecompetencies/corecompetenciesbusiness

This resource from ALA's BRASS Education Committee lists specific core resources that would be found in a small to mid-sized public library.

Business Books: Core Collections and More

http://businesslibrary.uflib.ufl.edu/businessbooks

The University of Florida's business guides were pointed to earlier in this chapter, but their Business Books category is especially noteworthy in terms of collection development. It lists titles found in their stacks and considered core for a number of business reference areas. Also keep in mind that it's never a bad idea to snoop around other library sites to see what their collections look like. The New Books at Baker Library from Harvard was noted earlier, too, but it doesn't hurt to find out what other big business school programs' libraries have as well as public libraries and/or an institution similar in size and scale to your own.

Outstanding Business Reference Titles

http://rusa.metapress.com/home/main.mpx

This is another useful resource from BRASS, this time from their Business Reference Sources Committee. They publish their list of selected outstanding titles (including significant updates to important works) in the winter issue of *Reference and User Services Quarterly*. The link here points to the main RUSQ site. You can search for *outstanding business* to find the current and past lists.

Sudden Selector's Guide to Business Resources by Robin Bergart and Vivian Lewis (Chicago: ALCTS/American Library Association, 2007)

www.alastore.ala.org/detail.aspx?ID=2319

This slim volume contains a wealth of great advice for anyone without a business background who is nevertheless faced with collection development responsibilities in the business discipline. It highlights key publishers, associations, and other useful resources to help the new business selector learn how to build and maintain their collection. Some of the same resources are covered within the pages of Making Sense of Business Reference, too, but the Sudden Selector's Guide to Business Resources focuses nicely and succinctly on the topic of business reference within the context of collection development.

Journal of Business and Finance Librarianship

www.haworthpress.com/store/product.asp?sku=J109

A great journal for getting reviews of new resources and just keeping on top of the business research scene. Consider contacting their book or database review editor if you'd like to get your business reference publishing feet wet by writing a review.

Business Information Review

http://bir.sagepub.com

Another great resource for keeping up on business reference resources and strategies and another potential outlet for you if you're interested in reviewing business-related items for publication.

Choice

www.cro2.org

Considered a vital collection development tool for academic librarians in all subject areas, Choice reviews books and databases relevant to business reference topics as well.

Information Today

www.infotoday.com/IT/default.asp

This publication is geared toward information professionals and often has the latest news on what's going on behind the scenes with various database vendors and business reference products. Information Today Inc., which publishes *Information Today*, also publishes a number of other really useful publications like *Online* (www.infotoday.com/online/) and *Searcher* (www.infotoday.com/searcher/), and the newsletter *Information Advisor* (www.informationadvisor.com).

BUSINESS REFERENCE GUIDES AND GENERAL SEARCHING HANDBOOKS

While this book will highlight some key business reference resources and should serve as a handy guide for some business reference tips and pointers, as I mentioned, it is not a compendium of all things business reference. In fact, we've really only covered the tip of the iceberg. Nor does this book focus in depth on database and online search strategies. A good general reference book sometimes can't be beat. Here are some staples, at least a few of which should be in most large libraries' business reference collections:

> *Strauss's Handbook of Business Information: A Guide for Librarians, Students, and Researchers*, 3rd ed., by Rita W. Moss (Westport, CT: Libraries Unlimited, 2012)
>
> *The Basic Business Library: Core Resources*, The Basic Business Library: Core Resources and Services, 5th ed., edited by Eric Forte and Michael R. Oppenheim (Santa Barbara, CA: Libraries Unlimited, 2011)
>
> *Business: The Ultimate Resource*, 3rd ed., by Jonathan Law (London: A&C Black, 2011)
>
> *How to Find Business Information: A Guide for Businesspeople, Investors and Researchers*, by Lucy Heckman (New York: Praeger, 2011)
>
> *Research on Main Street: Using the Web to Find Local Business and Market Information*, by Marcy Phelps (Medford, NJ: CyberAge Books, 2011)
>
> *ALA Guide to Economics and Business Reference* (Chicago: American Library Association, 2011)
>
> *Encyclopedia of Business Information Sources*, 28th ed. (Farmington Hills, MI: Gale, 2011)
>
> *The Extreme Searcher's Internet Handbook: A Guide for the Serious Searcher*, 3rd ed., by Randolph Hock (Medford, NJ: CyberAge Books, 2009)
>
> *Librarian's Guide to Online Searching*, 2nd ed., by Suzanne S. Bell (Westport, CT: Libraries Unlimited, 2009)

The Skeptical Business Searcher: The Information Advisor's Guide to Evaluating Web Data, Sites, and Sources, by Robert Berkman (Medford, NJ: Information Today, 2004)

Industry Research Using the Economic Census: How to Find It, How to Use It, by Jennifer C. Boettcher and Leonard M. Gaines (Westport, CT: Greenwood Press, 2004)

Business Statistics on the Web: Find Them Fast—At Little or No Cost, by Paula Berinstein (Medford, NJ: CyberAge Books, 2003)

The Core Business Web: A Guide to Key Information Resources, edited by Gary W. White (New York: Haworth Information Press, 2003)

Business Information: How to Find It, How to Use It, 3rd ed., by Michael Halperin (Phoenix, AZ: Oryx Press, 2003)

International Business Information: How to Find It, How to Use It, 2nd ed., by Ruth A. Pagel and Michael Halperin (New York: AMACOM, 2000)

Business Information Sources, 3rd ed., by Lorna Daniells (Berkeley: University of California Press, 1993)

START MAKING SENSE!

- Sign up for BusLib and read what kinds of questions (and answers!) come through. Think of a stumper (or pick one from the appendix) and see what you find searching through the archives.
- Review the BRASS website and consider joining if you'd like to expand your network of fellow business reference enthusiasts.
- Explore the Special Library Association (SLA) Business and Finance website. Look into your state's chapter to see how active it is and what kinds of resources it offers.
- Pick one or two Google resources (e.g., Google Scholar, Google Patent, Google Maps) that you are less familiar with and try out some business reference–related searches.
- Look through the collection development questions and see how many you can answer about your collection.
- See if you own any of the guides or handbooks listed here, and, if you do, flip through them to familiarize yourself with the info they hold.
- Take a look through some of the library websites noted here and find inspiration for making improvements and adjustments to your own site.

12

BUSINESS REFERENCE WRAP-UP

A ND SO WE'VE reached the end of *Making Sense of Business Reference*. I really hope you've enjoyed working your way through this book and that it has helped you to make at least some sense of this complicated and sometimes intimidating topic. As I've mentioned earlier, no single book on any topic is going to make you an expert overnight, but I hope you now feel like you don't need to hide under the reference desk next time you're faced with a business reference question.

Here's what we've covered in a nutshell:

Business reference questions generally can be broken down into one or more of the following Core Four topics:

- Company information
- Industry information
- Investing/financial information
- Consumer information/business statistics

Business reference databases (and other resources) will generally cover one or more of the following:

- News/trade/research articles

- Company profiles
- Industry profiles
- Analyst reports
- Consumer information
- International information
- Directory information
- Raw (mostly financial/economic) data

A successful business reference interaction will involve identifying the core information being asked for and the type of source (or combination of sources) that will be likely to have it. Remember, a thorough reference interview is crucial, as is remembering the other secret business reference tip from the beginning of the book: not every business reference question, especially as asked, can be answered.

So, when faced with a business reference question, take a step back and examine it. Break it down and focus on those smaller pieces of the puzzle rather than searching for the entire holy grail. What is the patron really looking for? Which of the Core Four categories might be applicable and what types of resources might be of use? Start with your favorites or "the usual suspects," and be creative in your overall approach. Ask yourself, "Who cares?" Try to find clues along the way and use them to guide the rest of your research. Don't forget to leverage the reference and research skills you already have. Above all, don't be afraid to ask for help! Oh, and have fun while you're at it, too.

As I've mentioned, business reference is like any skill—it takes time and practice to become familiar with the resources and processes. And even the most seasoned of business researchers will tell you that they learn something new almost every day. All this learning doesn't take place in a bubble, so be sure to take advantage of the many resources that are out there to help you. Sign up for BusLib, take a look at some other business library sites, see what you can bring back to your library and incorporate into your own personal reference tool belt. And if it's a while before your next wave of business reference questions and you forget some of what you've learned here, don't hesitate to ask for assistance.

One of the best ways to stay sharp and keep some of these newly found skills honed is to be aware—business is going on all around you all the time, and you're a part of it. Whenever you fill your car with gas, buy groceries, take an airplane somewhere, go to the movies, or choose a health care or retirement plan, you are participating in the market. Maybe you're a shareholder. Maybe you're an employee. We are all consumers, and we are all some kind of demographic—and so much more, of course. Keep up on business news in the papers and in general, and try to recognize all of the business and economic activity going on around you. This shouldn't be hard—librarians and researchers are naturally curious. And now you know you don't have to be afraid of business just because it's business.

Just as one workout at the gym won't leave you with rock-hard abs, so too will it take time to build up your business reference muscles. The next time you are faced with a business reference challenge, think back to the beginning of this book when I reminded you of the skills you already possess, and don't get discouraged if it sometimes feels overwhelming. Start with the Core Four and build from there. You'll be running business reference marathons, or at least 5Ks, in no time!

START MAKING SENSE!

- Take a look at the Stumpers appendix now and see if some of the questions in there seem as intimidating as they did before you made your way through this book.
- Review what you've learned here—what are three things you know now that you didn't before reading this book?
- Set some time aside—make it an appointment in your calendar or carve it out in some other formal way—and explore two to three resources noted in the book that stood out to you for whatever reason. If you can do this on a regular basis, all the better.

STUMPERS

T THE BEGINNING of every online Business Reference workshop that I teach, I ask each student to submit a *stumper*—a business reference question that has them shaking their heads (or shaking in their boots!). At the end of each workshop, I ask the students to review the stumpers to see whether or not the questions still seem so daunting or confusing. This appendix contains a sampling of some of those tricky business reference questions as experienced by real librarians and researchers. Reviewing this Stumpers section will help you to know that you're not alone in your struggle with tough business reference questions! These are "real" questions from librarians and researchers just like you.

As you read through these, you may notice that, more often than not, I don't actually answer the questions but rather provide some tips and ideas for how to approach them. I hope that for the most part these responses contain sound advice, but I imagine that there are at least a few where I've overlooked some obvious (to you) sources or where new resources have appeared on the landscape that didn't exist at the time (these questions span a good five years or so). My responses will lean heavily on my personal preferences as far as databases and search strategies go, and I readily admit that there are likely many different ways each of these questions can be approached. Hopefully I haven't misguided anyone through my own lack of understanding on some of these topics—they are stumpers, after all!

STUMPERS: COMPANIES

Q: My university offers a "green" MBA, so I get a lot of questions around this. One question that I remember was how to find all the green businesses in the San Francisco Bay Area. Is that even possible?

A: There's no easy way that I know of to identify green companies. You'll want to work with the students to have them define what they mean by *green* and then figure out how to use whatever criteria they come up with to build a list. There are some sites out there that focus on green business, but many are commercial and are just a lot of ads. The Business.gov site has a handy green business page: www .business.gov/manage/green-business/. One of their links points to case studies of successful businesses who went green. I'd also suggest doing some article searching to see if you can glean some local examples that way and, of course, look for local groups focused on this topic.

Ask yourself, "Who cares?" Maybe there is a version of a green consumer group or business association in SF. Is there any kind of regulatory agency that gives the equivalent of "green seals of approval"? This is the kind of brainstorming you'll want to do with the students. At the very least, you can determine what kinds of databases you might have that would provide a list of local companies (you'll have to narrow it down somehow—maybe by size or number of employees) that the students could skim through and follow up on to see if they would be considered green.

Also consider building a guide to the topic. Not only will it be useful to you and the students, you can also use it to highlight the library's services to the new program! Vanderbilt has put together a LibGuide on "Green and Sustainable Businesses." I don't think any of the resources can help you narrow down to a local number of green businesses, but some of the resources under the Websites tab might be useful for you in: http://libguides.owen.vanderbilt.edu/greenbusiness.

Q: I am not sure if my topic is clear enough. I know several databases where I can find company profiles (Business Source Premier, Hoover's, Mergent, Plunkett, etc.). However, I am often struggling to find data about subsidiaries, particularly if the subsidiary has a different name than the parent company. For instance, today I was looking for the designer Michael Kors and his company, to find out whether it is a subsidiary to Estée Lauder. Is there a way to find out who owns whom?

A: Finding info on subsidiary companies is hard. You've already discovered that most databases take the easy way out and only cover top-level parent (and sometimes only publicly traded parent) companies. Even if you're in a database that might give you some info on a subsidiary, the parent companies themselves are not required to break out their information by subsidiary. So, in your example, Estée Lauder doesn't have to say what's going on specifically with each of their 921 companies (yes, 921 and counting—at least according to a quick OneSource search). Your best bet with subsidiaries (and/or private companies) is to hunt for information in article databases and online. And you'll see that databases like Hoover's and OneSource are often useful to at least identify who is a subsidiary and who is a parent (but even then, it's not always straightforward).

Q: I would like to know how to find a company's market share for a certain product.

A: Another "top 10" business stumper. People are often looking for market share of a company (or, relatedly, market size of product x). One thing to know is that you're never going to find an *exact* number. Whatever you can find will be an estimate and it will be based on a certain definition of the market itself and the players.

This is one of those questions to ask yourself, "Would I want my competitors to know this if I were this company?" The answer is no. Plus, companies aren't required to break out their sales by product or market. They only have to report total sales. So, if you want to know the market share of Home Depot in the lumber market, you're going to have to dig for articles, find estimates of total market sizes, pointers to other players, and anything you can find that specifically mentions Home Depot and lumber. You may hit the jackpot and find a trade journal that reports the top players in lumber and their market share, but this is not something you should count on. Also, be careful of market info you do find—how is the source defining the lumber market? Are you getting market share as a percentage? A percentage of what (in other words, what is the total market size that they have a share of)?

For some products, markets, and companies, this kind of research gets even trickier. Some good resources to start with are the *Market Share Reporter* and the *Business Rankings Annual* publications. (These are in print and online.)

Q: I have had difficulty finding the complete history and financial information on the private company L'Oréal Cosmetics (this was needed for fund-raising by a local nonprofit organization).

A: It's always harder to find information (of any kind) on private companies than it is for public companies.

There are a few resources that specialize in private companies (Ward's Business Directory of U.S. Private and Public Companies is one.) But even in these specialized directories, you'll only get cursory info—at the most, expect to find maybe a sales estimate.

For larger companies, even when private (or subsidiary), you may have some luck in doing an article search and piecing together some info. Again, financials are really off the table. You'll have to see what kinds of estimates you can find and see what you can do with them creatively—some tips include identifying similar companies/competitors that are public and "stealing" from them (obviously, you won't have exact numbers, but you might have a good idea of approximate expenditures and profits). Also, if they are a big enough player in their industry (as L'Oréal would be), you can look for industry overviews and other profiles to see if those mention your company or give additional info.

So, my advice when you know you're dealing with a private company is to readjust your (and your patrons') expectations and then set to digging in the hopes that you can build something. Give yourself time to do this and be as creative as possible in your searching.

Q: Any suggestions about finding businesses that fit poorly into the standard numerical classification systems (e.g., the SIC and the NAICS)? A while ago, a customer came to the business reference desk looking for "a charting service for small-cap stocks." Now, using the NAICS-2002, that's "523999—Miscellaneous Financial Investment Activities," but that's something of a catch-all category. Finding the charting services among all the other financial odds-and-ends generated by a ReferenceUSA search using that number would be a real needle-in-a-haystack activity.

A: One thing I've mentioned is to not get too hung up on the codes themselves. They're enticing because they seem so exact and like they hold the answers to a particularly elusive industry question, but they're really just one small tool that may or may not be helpful.

Also, if you're trying to identify companies, most online directories will use either SIC or NAICS codes in some way, but these are by no means comprehensive or exact. And remember that companies can do more than one thing, so you may need to broaden your search and then try to see if the companies you find also do the more specific task at hand.

Finally, if you or your patron can identify (or know of) at least one or two companies that fit the bill, use what you can find on them to point you toward additional information. For example, look them up in your directory by name and see what codes or other industry keywords are assigned. You may find that the NAICS code that you found isn't used at all. Whenever possible, it's best to start out this way rather than to try to identify a code first and hope that it is being used consistently (especially when it's one of the "Miscellaneous" ones).

Q: A patron requested contact information for the board of directors for Lowe's. I easily found their names, but was clueless about finding addresses or telephone numbers for them. The patron didn't want to go through the customer service website for Lowe's, as she had already done that and received no response. Where should I have looked?

A: Contact info for that level of executive/board director can be hard to find (gee, I wonder why they don't want to be easily contacted?). Many databases, if they include executive information, don't give out information beyond executives' names and where they went to school. If contact info is available, it's often only available for a fee. So you're not overlooking some big source where these kinds of things are kept. If you're lucky, you might be able to find a few e-mail addresses of some of the employees, then try to figure out if there's a particular naming structure (e.g., John Jones is jjones@lowes.com or john_jones@lowes.com) and try to wing it. I did some quick searching in their annual report (not an "@" sign in it) and in a few other places and didn't see anything. Your patron may just have to keep badgering the customer service lines (and hopefully not you).

Q: This is a common stumper—and probably indicative of the fact that my coworker and I are very new to business reference! We struggle with helping students discover the management structure of a particular company. Often they have been assigned to find more than just the company's executives (which we can locate using a number of resources), and if the information is not available through the company's website, we're usually stumped. I'd be interested to hear if anyone has further suggestions for this type of information.

A: This is one of *those* questions . . . the kind that are hard to find the answer to because of their proprietary nature. A company's management structure is sometimes something that they want to keep under wraps, as they consider it part of their competitive edge and don't want to make it easy for their competitors to copy. Everyone wants to know what the most effective organizational structure is.

As an interesting illustration, I found this article from an old Harvard Business School newsletter called "How Org Charts Lie": http://hbswk.hbs.edu/archive/4171.html. If you look at the first org chart used as an example, it says, "Note: This example has been substantially disguised at the request of the organization." And if you look at the actual example, there's not much to it at all!

My suggestion when it comes to these kinds of org chart/management structure requests is to do what you can to find out titles of key executives and/or departments and use those to help you craft a possible version of an org chart, knowing that there will be a lot of holes and possibly mistakes in hierarchy.

That said, there are some resources, both free and fee, that offer some examples of large companies or other ideas. Here is a Rutgers subject guide that I found by googling *org charts library guide site:.edu*: www.libraries.rutgers.edu/rul/rr_gateway/research_guides/busi/company.shtml#H.7.

Finally, it never hurts to do an article search, and you can look for *(org chart or organizational chart or management structure) and best practice* or similar terms.

Q: This is an especially important question because we offer a course that requires students to analyze companies and their marketing budgets. They then have to compare this information with competitors and analyze how the company may redistribute or revise their marketing budgets (along with a bunch of other stuff). The problem is that students always seem to want to do private companies, and I can't get it through their heads that this makes things a lot harder for them. Maybe we can devise a way to ease that pain somewhat?

A: This will definitely be a painful process if the students want to use exact numbers for a private company's marketing budget. Even a public company won't necessarily break out their spending in this area.

Gather together some resources on marketing budgets in general and talk with the professor to find out what kind of information the students are being presented with in class. Then work with them to use what they know about marketing budgets (what they're composed of—advertising, giveaways, etc.), help them find some info on the private company (*maybe* you can find a total revenue estimate), and help them extrapolate. This page (from a company that looks to be trying to sell their marketing services to small businesses) actually has some pretty good breakdowns of percentages: www.imageworksstudio.com/client-lounge/articles-tips/setting-a-marketing-advertising-budget.html.

Honestly, for this kind of assignment, even for the public companies it's going to be a little tricky, although you'd certainly be able to get a better overall breakdown of their finances than you will for private companies. If nothing else, maybe you can work with the professor and find out more about what the learning goals for this assignment are. Maybe you can get them to assign specific, publicly traded companies or limit them to public companies.

Q: I am new to business reference and have specialized in medical librarianship. However, I am going to put the business hat on now. Apple Computer is known for their high-quality products. How much of their manufacturing is done in the United States versus their manufacturing process—particularly in China? Perhaps, what is different about their manufacturing steps/locations that make them different from those of other companies that produce Windows products?

A: Oooh—good one. I would start with some open Internet searching to see what clues I could find and then take those into an article search and maybe even analyst reports if you have access to those. A quick Google search for *Apple "manufacturing process"* turned up a lot of insider blogs and things like that where you're sure to find some clues. A similar search on *Apple "manufacturing facilities"* details the secrecy at their Asian plants but also lists some of their major suppliers. You could search for articles on Apple and China in general, too. You could also broaden your search to look for *computers "best practice" manufacturing* to see what comes up—it's not likely you'll find head-to-head comparisons just due to the propriety of the process, but you never know what will turn up. And don't forget to search through Apple annual reports and other company documents to see what they note in those. [Note: This question was asked before the recent spate of news coverage focused on Apple's manufacturing practices in China. A search like the one described here performed in mid-2012 and beyond will likely turn up even more resources.]

Q: I sort of feel like this shouldn't stump me, but nevertheless: how do you determine what somebody's business model is? I think I understand the definition of a business model (how operations are set up to actually make money), but it's hard to go from there to actually figuring out what that is for a specific company. There are sometimes freelance research projects that involve reporting on the business plan of some company (usually private and somewhat obscure), and I would like to be comfortable taking those on.

A: Actually, in many cases, a company's business model *is* intended to stump you. At the very least, they don't want anyone to know what it is (so that their competitors can't copy it). Often your best bet will be to try to find whatever kind of information you can on the company in question and go from there—search for articles, search online, take a look at their website. Maybe you can find some listings for various departments or get a sense of their overall corporate culture. Alternatively, you could work with the patron to get them to focus on specific aspects of a business model—finance, IT, HR, and so on—and look for things on best practice and the like. But there is no easy way that I'm aware of to go and find a specific company's specific business models. You could look for general information on business models (vs. business plans) and see if any clues turn up.

Q: This is one of those things that looks as though it should be a piece of cake: list the top thirty employers (by number of employees) in three hundred cities (e.g., Chicago, New York, Milwaukee, Pittsburgh).

Crain's Chicago Business publishes a list of Chicago's twenty-five largest employers annually. Crain's New York has not done such a list since 2006. Some of the other Crain's regional publications do similar lists for a county or a whole metro area but not for just the city proper. Help!

A: I also thought of the Crain's publications when I first saw this list, but for three hundred cities I knew they'd likely fall short.

For this kind of question, I think you'd have to resort to some kind of directory database, like ReferenceUSA or OneSource. You can limit by geography (just city, if you want, and they also offer zip codes and metro areas and other options). You can also screen by number of employees and by sales. It's a little tricky to sort ReferenceUSA before exporting your results, and you're only allowed to export fifty at a time, so you will have to get a little creative.

An easier database that would allow this kind of searching is the OneSource Global Business Browser—you can do the same kind of screening and sort by number of employees on the fly and then just export the top thirty.

If you don't have these kinds of screening databases, you'd have to resort to specialized resources, like the Crain's lists, for each of the local areas. Then you'd be stuck (a) hoping to find a source like that and then (b) hoping that it ranked by number of employees (and not just sales).

Along these lines, one potential local resource might be something like a chamber of commerce or other local or state group that focuses on employers in their area. You could contact local SBA offices for suggestions here. It might not get you the top employers by city, but at least for the area.

Q: I've gotten several questions regarding the logistics issues and/or supply chain management issues of a specific company. Normally, I'd go to sources like Business Source Complete and ABI/Inform, but I never find more than an article or two (usually out of date). Any ideas of strategies or better sources?

A: You're doing the right thing by looking for articles. The reason you're not finding too much is simply because the logistics and supply chain of a company is considered proprietary/secret. You can do a few more things to look for info—try looking for articles on the industry that the company operates in and *(supply chain or logistics or scm)* (and any other related terms you can think of). You can also add *"best practices"* and at least try to figure out who is considered to be doing it right and extrapolate from there. You can also look up your company and *(suppliers or distributors)* and see if you can come up with some relationships. You can look for trade journals in the industry area of your company or supply chain publications (sometimes these will come up in your general article search; other times it helps to start at an industry or supply chain publication and drill down from there). There's a database from Mergent called Mergent Horizon that focuses on supply chain, although it's not totally comprehensive (it can't really be since some of this info is internal to the company), but it's something. Also, it never hurts to look to see if a library out there has a guide on supply chain (try a Google search for *"supply chain" and library and site:.edu*). If you find some tricks that work, put them together in your own guide and spread the love!

STUMPERS: INDUSTRY

Q: One of our agribusiness marketing classes gets an assignment to create a business plan for a small business. Sometimes it is fairly easy for me to get them information, but last year one student wanted to find information about trends, market share, and so on of businesses that clean/wash agricultural machinery, and I was stuck.

A: This is one of those "niche-industry" types of questions where you'll want to maintain your sanity with a few tips. Look for articles and identify companies that participate in whatever industry you're looking into. In this case, you might have to play around with the terminology and/or broaden your scope to vehicle washing in general, or maybe looking into truck washing and similar businesses. Keep in mind that many of these companies will be small and/or private, and/or do more than one thing (i.e., they don't just wash agricultural machinery). If you can find some companies that specialize in this, take those names into a directory database and see if you can find them and use whatever kinds of descriptions the database has for them (industry codes, etc.) to identify similar companies. As I've mentioned before, when in doubt, ask yourself, "Who cares?" In this case, maybe that's either people who either use agricultural machinery or maybe even people who make agricultural machinery (and even if they don't "care," per se, finding out more about them might still give you some info to use). I did a quick Google search for *agricultural machinery association* and found a Farm Equipment Manufacturers Association. They might be able to point you to data about numbers of pieces of equipment, cleaning needs and practices, and so on. You never know unless you call. Remember that, with any business plan, it's often difficult to get down to all the pieces of detail that a patron will be asking for (like market share, total numbers of businesses, etc.), but some of these tips might help.

Q: What information technologies (both hardware and software) are companies implementing in beverage production?

A: Good stumper! This is the kind of question where you'll have to start broadly by identifying what you can on the industry overall—within some of those reports, you will likely find some discussion of technology. Don't forget an article search— try some of the business article databases (like Business Source Complete). Play around with your terminology and see what kinds of clues you find along the way—remember that you might need to be flexible. You may need to look for *soft drinks and/or beer or milk,* etc., instead of just *beverages,* and you'll likely want to try *software or hardware or technology* and other variations of those terms to start finding things. You may also find that you need to break out your search into areas of beverage production—the beverage itself, packaging, distribution. And a quick online search for the beverage industry will point you to some of the trade journals out there—check those for special technology reports or columns or other ideas on how to adjust your search.

Q: A student recently requested information on the most popular type of music, rock, county, R&B, blues, etc. He was going to use the information for his statistics class, actually.

A: Hmmm . . . here's a question where we'd have to step back and take a look at what the student means by "popular" and maybe even genre. Does he want sales? Of CDs? Downloads? Concert tickets? What's played on the radio? Also, if he needs it for a statistics class, what kind of format does the data need to be in? And how many years of data does he need? Almost always, it's a good idea to get some clarification before heading off willy-nilly on a data quest like this.

My first thought when I saw this was that *Billboard* or perhaps some other trade publication might have this kind of info. Of course, getting the info in a format that the student can use is a different story. The Recording Industry Association of America (RIAA) may also have data. In doing a quick Google search on music sales data, I stumbled across a paper that just coincidentally focused on statistics: http://cobweb.ecn.purdue.edu/~malcolm/yahoo/Chon2006%28SongPredictions%29 .pdf. You could look to see what kinds of sources they used for that or for other, similar papers.

Also in digging around, I was reminded that Nielsen (the same people that bring you Nielsen ratings) has an entertainment division and a product called Soundscan that tracks music sales (and other products that track radio, etc.). Of course, that's going to cost. A lot.

So . . . first clarify what the student really needs, then start hunting around for clues to sources and drill down from there. Remember to look for trade publications and associations and look for similar research and track back from their sources. Not the most straightforward process, but that's why it's a stumper, right?

Q: Raisins are big in California's Central Valley, and I've gotten a few questions about the economics of the raisin industry, specifically in this area. I've had a hard time finding info on anything more specific than "grapes."

A: A quick Google search for *raisin industry* points me to a California raisin industry association (www.calraisins.org/about/the-raisin-industry/) and also a report from Cornell on "The US and World Situation: Raisins" (http://usda .mannlib.cornell.edu/usda/fas/raiswm//2000s/2007/raiswm-07-02-2007.pdf) that cites the USDA as its source.

These are the kinds of clues that I'd start to look for—industry associations, tracking back where data is coming from, etc. I'd try to see if any local university has a department or expert in this area, too—there may be a dedicated research center or something like that.

Also, if the questions come up frequently enough, you might want to consider building a guide—it will help you and your patrons learn about "the raisin situation."

Q: I had a patron ask about the market share of kayak rentals in our county (Santa Clara). I couldn't find anything that would break down to that specific market.

A: Yup . . . that's a stumper all right. More often than not, your patrons won't care about any of the industries that you have nice, packaged data for. Instead, they'll want to know about kayaks. In your county. Broken out by purchases and rentals. By day of the week. And color. Just joking (sort of). As you've already discovered, this kind of level of detail is tricky. Most of the time you're going to have to do what you can to come up with an overall market size (and in this case, you might not even be able to get it down to kayaks; you might only find info on boating in general or kayaks and canoes) and then play around with the numbers. Think creatively about the industry itself, too, and don't get totally bogged down with *kayaks and "Santa Clara County"*. Think about outdoor recreation, look for local boating groups, local companies, etc. and see if they can provide any clues (and talk with your patron and involve her in brainstorming). Be open to state, regional, etc. data, too. In the end, you may not have much in the way of specific numbers by county, but you might have enough to help the patron paint a pretty robust picture.

Q: A high-energy, high-achieving entrepreneur who is always looking for the next excellent opportunity heads one of my companies. He's a fascinating guy. At one point a few months ago, he explained to me that if he doesn't know everything about what a producer within an agricultural sector does, he wouldn't know how to create a product/process to make that producer's life easier and more profitable. Here's an almost verbatim comment: "If I don't know what it takes for an almond farmer to get his almonds into the store, I can't create a machine that will help him do it more efficiently." As a result, he wants to create a database of agricultural industry statistics (margins, production rates, annual yields) to help him. I told him I'd work on providing him the classifications to use, and he'll come up with what statistics he'd like.

Which leads me to my problem: I don't really know where I will go to find the answers to his questions. As I noted above, he'll be looking for data on annual yields, prices, margins, historical averages, all having to do with all agriculture sectors including crop, livestock, processing, and distribution.

I've spent some time at the USDA and National Agricultural Statistics Service websites, but navigating them is not easy. Help!

A: As you've already discovered, this is a really detailed, involved question. Likely you're going to have to break it down into some smaller pieces and figure out how to tackle each. For the overall life cycle of an almond (or any other kind of similar agricultural product), I'd try to identify experts and industry journals and start calling around and digging. You'll also want to think of the terminology and topics that would be related to "getting an almond into the store." Supply chain? Distribution? Logistics? What commodity market are almonds traded/priced on? Identify associations—there will be lots of state associations in the regions where almonds are grown, I'm thinking. And probably a national one, too (or at least a national "nut" association).

In the end, some of this information isn't "database ready." It will come from people—"experts" who either grow the crops or trade the crops or sell the crops or some combination. Or there are likely academic experts out there, at least in the area of commodities like almonds (try adding that term to your search—*commodity and almonds*). You might have to bring in someone like that to help with a project like this, or perhaps start a database of experts rather than data. An expert can give you a much broader picture and prioritize some of the information for you in a way that hunting for data on your own won't allow. She can also speak to things like up- and downstream channels. What are some of the factors that influence the growing of almonds (farm machinery prices, gas prices, fertilizer, weather) and what else can almonds be used for besides eating whole (almond butter, body products, etc.)?

This is all just off the top of my head, but I think if you can come up with some of the relevant associations and publications and identify some people to call, that might make the next steps easier. Be careful not to allow the requester too much latitude in choosing "the statistics he'd like." Try to present the info in terms of "statistics he can get" and then brainstorm ways he can use that data to tell him what he wants to know (and, again, enlist the help of an expert or two to assist in determining what kinds of statistics are available).

Q: I am looking for any kind of index to compare the most current cost of manufacturing machinery/autos in America vs. China, Japan, or other countries. Do you have any sources to help me with this? Our business databases offer production numbers and sales per country but not cost of production. I even called the Center for Automotive Research, and they were not helpful. Short of searching for articles, are there any other ideas? I am also interested in finding cost information for ingredients that are used in the production of plastic. The ingredients I am specifically interested in are used as fillers. These items are clay, calcium carbonate, mica, wood flour, and glass. I am doing research to compare the cost of these materials with the cost of a new green product to see if they are comparable in cost. Is there a source that will provide a cost for these items, preferably given per pound?

A: This stumper was giving me some déjà vu, because I remember working with a team of students looking into electric vehicles who were looking for a breakdown of what it cost to build a car (by individual make and model, of course).

One thing I would also try to do is look into the plastics manufacturing/production angle of the question without any connection to the auto industry. Articles and associations might have some info on costs and maybe an overview of the process. I noticed that in IBISWorld there is a handy Plastic Products Miscellaneous Manufacturing in the U.S. report that might also have some good info. For the individual items the patron was referring to, you could try a check in Thomasnet.com. I see that they have a plastics/rubber category. You can also search on terms like *mica* and get a list of companies and see if there are any clues—if nothing else, you might be able to contact a few (or give the list to your patron to contact) and see if anyone there is willing to talk more about whether their company supplies auto manufacturers. They may also be able to point you to a resource for tracking costs per pound for the various resources.

It sounds like you were on track with identifying the Center for Automotive Research. I did a Google search for *"auto manufacturing" cost per pound* (just to see what might come up) and was pointed to this recent article from a chemical industry company: "Plastic Grows in Auto Manufacturing" (www.icis.com/Articles/2010/06/02/9364337/plastic-grows-in-auto-manufacturing.html). It mentions the Center for Automotive Research, too, and contains a handy chart with a reference to the American Composites Manufacturers Association and the (even more promising-sounding) Automotive Composites Alliance. The article also references things like IHS Global Insights that might be worth digging in to, depending on how far your patron wants to take this.

Here's my original reply to the student looking for the cost breakdown of building a car, for what it's worth:

It's harder than I thought to get a breakdown of the cost of building a car, especially down to the individual manufacturer, but there is some info in the IBISWorld database in the "Car and Automobile Manufacturing in the US" report (once you're in IBIS, do a "Find on page" for *automobile*). If you go into the Industry Conditions section you'll see some charts. There are other IBIS reports that might be of use to you (but none that I could find that gave a nice cost breakdown, unfortunately). If you go to the main page of IBIS and search in the "Find an industry by keyword or a company name" box for *electric cars*, you'll see some additional titles.

This column from *Forbes* is a little dated (2005), but it mentions some of the costs of car building that are tangential to the actual nuts and bolts and metal: www.forbes.com/2005/12/22/chrysler-auto-industry-cz_jf_1227flint.html.

And there's this article from *Businessweek* on the race to build really cheap cars (from 2007): www.businessweek.com/magazine/content/07_17/b4031064.htm.

Q: We offer several different MBAs. The liaison is a librarian in our Public Services group, so I get the questions/information needs thirdhand. In the courses, the students are developing business plans, and many are looking at businesses that have a focus on emerging technologies, such as biosensors. We've got one or two databases with industry info, but it's the traditional industry information. What the students are looking for is industry information in emerging industries and/or technologies. And that's where we get a little stumped.

A: One great resource for this kind of data is the Encyclopedia of Emerging Industries. It's also available as a print resource.

For other emerging industry research, go back to the tried-and-true article search and try to identify trade journals, and the like. There is a trade association for almost everything, even when it is fairly new and emerging.

Another good source to at least identify whether or not someone is tracking the emerging industry you're looking for is MarketResearch.com. It will point you to fee-based (very expensive) reports, but you can at least see what's out there. Also, don't forget to think of all the different ways your industry may be described to make sure you're searching comprehensively.

Q: A customer came in and wanted a list of all the companies in North Carolina that make supplies for furniture upholsterers.

A: The challenging part is narrowing things down based on all the different types of upholstery that are available.

Sometimes business reference questions are so specific it's easy to feel like there's no way you're going to find anything. And then you start to dig and realize that there's a lot more than you expected, but it's making it harder. Like, does the patron want actual upholstery manufacturers? Or people who supply them? With what? With machines to sew the upholstery? With needles and thread to go in the machines? With special lotion to rub on the upholstery? With dyes for the upholstery? With animal skins and other synthetics? Sigh . . . and I don't even know anything about upholstery. I'm just guessing here.

But, I will tell you that the first thing I thought of when I heard this question was the Thomas Register (www.thomasnet.com). You may even have a set of these giant green books on your reference shelves. The Thomas Register is essentially a catalog of catalogs of companies that supply manufacturers with all kinds of widgets and gadgets.

I did a search for *upholstery* limited to North Carolina and got a few companies that look like they manufacture upholstery. But then over on the right, I saw a list of "Related Categories" like fabrics, cleaners, edgings, tacks, nails, thread—all for upholstery. These may not all be related to North Carolina, but sometimes you'll find that you need to open up your scope with questions like these.

You've got some leads now with this and can either follow up by contacting an upholstery company (maybe you can find someone who can give you info), or at least some newfound knowledge of the upholstery industry that you didn't have before.

And don't forget to try to identify any trade associations or journals related to upholstery. These can be gold mines of info.

Q: I get questions for industry-related competitor/competitive analysis when there is a new product and researchers want to know what the market is for it. Or they want a list of all the major companies in an industry, and how much each spent in a certain area. They might be looking for competitors, or potential partners.

I was just asked today to help figure out how to do competitive analysis of a science-related market—information on existing technologies and companies. I don't know if I will be doing all the searches and finding all the information for them, since they are sending more info.

I find the terminology in this area so confusing. I just looked up the terms my client used—*competitive intelligence, competitive analysis*—and there are so many related words. So to begin with, I don't know what my client is asking for. I need to learn what questions to ask to figure that out, and which resources to go to.

A: First off, don't get thrown by the terminology. Whether you call it *competitive intelligence* or *competitive analysis* or just plain old *business research,* what they really want is to know how to make the next big thing and how to beat their competitors at it. This isn't the most straightforward process, and there are reasons for this—companies don't want to share this kind of information. Be careful not to get so caught up in the terminology related to *competitive intelligence* that you end up including it in your search terms. More likely than not, material that will provide insight into a market or company will not self describe as "competitive intelligence," so adding those extra terms will just throw your search off.

Talking your patrons through some of the search process and helping to manage their expectations of what you will likely (and likely not) be able to find will be your first step. Again, make sure you get them to clarify, and also try to get them to partner with you in part of the search—if nothing else, get them to talk about the industry and any other clues that might be of use to you. This isn't showing any kind of lack of knowledge, but rather trying to make the most of what you have available. Spin it that you are turning to them for their expertise in the industry and then take that to fuel your expertise in the area of researching.

Q: A type of question that poses frequent problems is a "supply chain question." Here are two examples:

(1) A student wanted to know the structure of the gaming industry (specifically hardware and consoles) in the United States, in particular mapping the route a product takes from conception to consumer.

(2) Another student wanted to know the steps in the construction and sale of a chair (from lumber to chair).

One specific type of information they want to know is the cost of each step (e.g., how much is shipping).

A: These kinds of questions are tricky because they're so involved. For the gaming industry, it sounds like the student has some specific ideas in mind of what he wants to focus on. It definitely wouldn't hurt to dig around for articles or packaged reports on the gaming industry and skim them to see if they mention major companies involved. You could also ask the patron for some examples and then start searching for those companies or products (e.g., Sony PlayStation). Once you start to build your vocabulary and get some basic terms, you can work with the patron to help define the industry (does the he want to include online multiplayer roleplaying games, for example?). Mainly you need to keep in mind that this kind of research takes time.

Same for the steps in the construction and sale of a chair. This could have a few approaches. Maybe there are some specific terminologies for life cycles of a product that you can determine and then take into an article or Internet search. Maybe it would help to identify some of the manufacturers of this kind of product and work backward. I did some quick Google searching for *chair manufacturers and life cycle* and was seeing a few things that might lead to more clues—again, combine some online searching with an article search and follow up on any leads. If you're spinning your wheels, step back and try a new angle. The main answer is that there is no easy answer. It's what keeps us reference librarians employed.

Q: A patron was looking for annual revenue of luggage tags sales for 2005, 2006, and 2007. He said if that was too specific, to try annual revenue of promotional products for the same years.

Sales data such as this is always hard for me to find.

A: Oh, my . . . this is one of those questions that starts out kind of hard to start with, and then the "easier alternative" question is at least as hard or harder. In the first case, luggage tags, the question is *very* specific, and in the second case, promotional products, the question is way too broad. I'd want to grill the patron a little and find out what he was trying to use this info for and to get him talking about his research . . . Is he aware that luggage tags aren't always promotional? That promotional products would include everything from tote bags to bobbleheads to T-shirts to magnets to pens to foam fingers to . . . ?

This isn't to say you couldn't find info on both of these topics, but you'd really need to know where he's going with it, if only to help you keep your sanity.

If nothing else, know that product sales of specific items are almost always hard to find, even if they're for more definable products like MP3 players or refrigerators. In those examples, I'd look for a consumer electronics association or related trade journal and the same for home appliances to see if I could find some data. With luggage tags—well, maybe I'd start with a search in travel-related trade journals. It wouldn't hurt to look for articles that mention luggage tags. My guess is that there are no companies that make only luggage tags. But you may be able to find something that talks about leather companies using leftover scraps to make tags and other smaller products.

This is a tough one for sure. I hope you didn't think it was any shortcoming on your part that made the data hard to find!

Q: A patron was looking for information on the "big and tall" industry and wanted some statistics that would show if people are getting larger and what impact that will have on the athletic footwear industry. We looked at Statistical Abstracts in the health and nutrition area but (surprisingly, to me) didn't find anything on obesity or anything else that would suggest people have collectively gained or lost weight. Next we looked at Datamonitor Industry profiles, but there wasn't a report specifically about the athletic footwear industry or the "big and tall" industry, just the footwear industry in the United States. We finally found an interesting report on the athletic footwear industry by doing a Google search, but it wasn't clear right off if it included information about "big and tall."

A: Now the pressure is on! I think you were smart to check Statistical Abstracts to start—you really never know what you're going to find there (and I'm surprised, too, that there wasn't anything on obesity or weight, but maybe you need a more health-oriented resource for that kind of data) . . . speaking of obesity statistics, though, I'd want to step back at this point and determine what you're really looking for—the patron has a preconceived idea and is trying to link two things, obesity and its impact on the footwear industry (specifically athletic footwear). You can take these two ideas and brainstorm on related keywords and concepts and then take that into an article database to look for clues . . . for example, try searching in Business Source Complete for *shoes or footwear and obesity or weight or "big and tall" and trends or impact* (or something along those lines). I wouldn't specifically start looking for athletic footwear. You could even just start with a broader search for *"big and tall" or "plus size" and apparel or footwear and industry* to see what kinds of info you find . . . we know there must be something going on if there are retail stores that target larger men and women already.

Also, keep in mind that you may not find anything that combines your patron's two concepts of athletic footwear and "big and tall." That's their connection and maybe there's nothing out there (yet) on it . . . what you can help them do, though, is find what they can on the athletic shoe industry. Period. And the "big and tall" (and whatever other names there might be for it, which you'll discover as you dig) industry. Period. And then they can start to extrapolate and pull it together. If they want data on weight trends to support their idea, that can be looked for separately.

This parsing out of key concepts in your patrons' business reference questions is crucial, no matter what the specific topic. Especially with students, but really with any business reference patron, you'll often find that they are trying to find very specific information and are pursuing their search with a much too narrow scope to begin with. Step back, and help them step back, and break it into more manageable pieces.

Remember, you don't have to do all the research and then tell the patrons what you did or didn't find. It's totally reasonable to discuss some of these new strategies with them and then get them pointed toward some resources so that they can do the grunt work themselves! (Although, I admit, sometimes it's fun to dig in, too!)

Q: We don't handle business questions much at my desk, because we have a separate business research desk. However, we will have to answer a lot more of them in the future, when our desks are combined. One recent question that I found frustrating was about sales in the furniture industry in the 1920s. I was at a loss for how to answer that question and finally remembered that we have expert business librarians who could handle it. I hope to be able to answer that and other questions like it in the future.

A: Don't feel bad for feeling at a loss when it comes to questions like these! Even a seasoned business librarian will have to step back and take a deep breath before tackling a tricky historical industry question like this. Obviously, you'll want to talk to the student/patron and find out what's going on first. Is this a question for a business class? A history class? A furniture-making class? The answer may change the way you approach the question. With any tricky industry question, historical or not, I usually think "literature search" first and would probably go look for articles on *furniture or furnishings and industry and history or historical* and see what comes up. Also, don't forget that the *New York Times* in its full run is available online for free (or, with slightly better search interfaces, through some fee databases). You can find articles from the 1920s on furniture companies, perhaps. If there are big furniture maker names that come up who are still around, you can look for company histories to see what is said. And don't forget books—in the case of furniture, you may end up finding some in the arts section, but there may be some that cover the topic from an industrial point of view. And don't forget general history sources, as well. You could try some of those "decade by decade" books or other books that cover a little bit of everything about time periods and see what turns up. It might not be exactly what the patron is looking for, but who knows? It might be the perfect complement to other info you find. But, one last time, it's *not* the fact that you are the librarian in question here that makes this hard to answer. It's just that you got thrown by the word *industry* and the fact that the "real" business librarian wasn't available. Just give it a little time and creative thinking (and enlist the patron to help—keep them talking to see if they can offer additional keywords, etc.). You can handle this kind of question. Just don't let it see you sweat . . . these kinds of stumpers can smell fear!

Q: We had a patron who wanted to know the average cost of college bowl games for the last fifteen years.

A: This question *seems* straightforward at first, but I bet it becomes a little snarly as you search for info. I'd treat this like an industry question and start broadly and then drill down. Don't worry about the fifteen years of historical data at first. Instead, try to identify resources that cover college bowls from a financial perspective (easier said than done—you'll likely have to sift through a lot of articles that talk about football strategies). Try keywords like *college bowl and profit or revenue or finance*. You may want to even just find a source that profiles all of the college bowl games going back over time: is there a particular go-to source for college bowl history and data? And don't forget to go to each bowl's website (which you'll discover exists as you dig further into this topic). There may be reports from each organizing committee and information about sponsors, funding, and so on.

You'll also want to clarify with the patron what they mean by "cost." Ticket prices? Overall cost to produce? What if bowls don't "cost" anything and are actually profitable? Maybe they mean how much money is spent on bowl games (and what does this mean? Just ticket and food sales or also team paraphernalia?). As you can see, it can spiral. But stick to your guns and "get smart" on bowl games with a search for top-level sources and then go from there.

Q: Things that "stump" me probably aren't stumpers for anyone else. But here goes:

1. Can you find me a SWOT report for Under Armour? (Turns out they don't have one. But how to find it, and what does it really mean?)

2. What are the market shares for electric cars?

A: Ah, SWOT and market share . . . two ol' standby stumpers. Let's start with SWOT: first of all, have you been able to figure out what *SWOT* means? It's just a fancy business school acronym that stands for *strengths, weaknesses, opportunities, threats,* and it provides a framework for analysis (you can even SWOT yourself, if you're so inclined).

Some databases have content that includes handy SWOT analysis all done out for large public companies—Datamonitor reports (which you can find in the Business Source Complete and Marketline databases) often have SWOT, but not always. In fact, I just checked Business Source Complete and got all excited because there was a report for Under Armour, but in this case there is no SWOT section. That's just the way it is. And even if there is, that doesn't mean that your work (or the student's or the entrepreneur's) is done. With a little digging for articles and company profiles, you can build your own SWOT analysis, using the SWOT framework. What are the company's strengths and weaknesses? Any opportunities for growth or improvement in the industry it operates within? What about threats? This is the kind of stuff you can tell your patrons as you walk them through some of the resources that might help them with this (company profile databases, article databases). So, a prepackaged SWOT report might not exist out there on Under Armour, but that doesn't mean you're out of luck.

Market share questions for any industry are tricky. If you luck out, you might be able to find an article or a report that specifically lays out the size of the market and the share that you're looking for. Often, you kind of have to build it yourself. In this case, you'd want to define the market: U.S. automobiles? Global automobiles? North American cars, not including SUVs and minivans? Transportation in general? Don't worry too much about getting exactly specific—as you search around for information, you may find that you'll have to take what you can get—maybe you can find a North American automobile market size and the percentage that is for electric cars but your patron is looking for global. You can use what you've found for the United States to help you estimate a global number. For this kind of market (electric cars) you might luck out and find a full report that contains the data you need. Also, don't forget to ask yourself who cares about this topic and look for some industry associations or consumer groups to see what info they might have, too.

Q: This isn't a stumper as much as a question I think I answered at a pretty bare-bones level (maybe a type of stumper): "Where would I be able to get market information on U.S. sales of cosmetics? I am specifically looking at makeup (face and eye). Maybe creams and lipstick, too."

In response, I offered:

- NAICS code from census website
- Census information from the Industry Statistics Sampler (by searching cosmetics in the industry search box on the Economic Census [2007] page)
- A search in Business Source Complete and then selecting Market Research Reports
- A few related trade association sites

I think this is an OK start, but I would like to be able to offer more for this type of question.

A: These kinds of industry questions will come up frequently. You've done a good job here by identifying a NAICS code and especially by searching for market reports and identifying associations. Really, this is often the most you can do. I would also use Business Source Complete to search for articles to see what clues they may be able to provide. Also, as the question indicates, there are many ways to say "cosmetics," so you'll want to work with the patron to define what the industry is, keeping in mind that you'll want to be open to finding reports that aren't *exactly* what you are looking for. For example, cosmetics is often part of health and beauty, but this might also include shampoo and soap. Think aloud with your patron to get him involved in the brainstorming process and explain that there's no one simple way to pull all of the data and info he wants. And don't rule out an open Internet search—google some of your terms and see what starts to come up. If you keep getting sites trying to sell you makeup, add terms like *industry* or *market size* and the like. You can also take your search into Google Scholar. You may run across an expensive market report that looks exactly right but that you don't have access to. You can still take a look at the abstract and possibly glean some market size numbers or other data. If nothing else, use some of the terms from the report in your article and report searching in other databases. Another way to approach this is to identify some known players in the industry and look for company information. (Not that this is always straightforward, either—the companies can be private, they might be part of a big conglomerate, etc.) Be on the lookout for clues in all your searching and then return with some new keywords as your vocabulary develops. You should stumble across a number of resources that your patron can use to build his own report. And when all of this searching and re-searching starts to overwhelm you and the patron, just remind them that this is why consultants get paid a lot of money!

STUMPERS: FINANCE AND INVESTING

Q: I would like to ask you a question about market capitalization. I looked up this term in Investorwords.com and got the definition, but it did not say how to evaluate one company's market cap versus another. Is a bigger number always better? Morningstar shows TBL's market cap at $915 million and the industry average as $4,100 million. This is a big difference! My first thought was that the industry average is better, but looking at the ratings for financial health, TBL was given a B and the industry average is C+. So, can you help me to understand these numbers/ratings?

A: I will first remind you that I'm in no way a stock or finance expert. I had to go and look this up myself: www.fool.com/investing/general/2005/05/03/market-cap-explained.aspx.

It talks about how you can consider the market cap of a company sort of like an approximate price tag—essentially, because it is based on share price, it is reflecting what investors believe to be the "value" of the company. So, bigger numbers are good, and it will make sense that an entire industry will be larger than one company in it.

But people can speculate and their sense of value can be off (think of the dot-com and real estate busts), so it's just one quick eyeball way to get a sense of a company's standing in the overall market. It could change with the sale of stock later this afternoon. Whatever happens, it's just one measure of a company, and you wouldn't want to solely look at that number to base investing decisions on. (And keep in mind that only public companies will have market cap.) There are lots of other measures, including many of those industry and company ratios that would give you additional insight and bring in additional pieces of the company (like their debt) that would give you a more robust picture.

Q: Anything related to finance is a stumper for me, but for our purposes: "How can I find a stock (or was it bond?) that has had its rating changed in the past three months?"

A: Yikes! I can relate. And I can tell you that even though somehow I always wind up as the liaison to the finance department in whatever job I have, these kinds of questions never get any easier. You were probably being asked about bonds, which get rated as a reflection, basically, of how likely the ratings agency thinks it is that the company that took out the bond (aka borrowed money) will pay it back. (That's my *limited* understanding, at least.) There are three big bond ratings agencies: Standard & Poor's, Fitch, and Moody's (sometimes called Mergent). (Of course, there are also things called preferred stock which I think also get rated—but let's assume they mean bonds, since those are more likely.)

Now the fun really starts: Which rating agency does the patron need? Do they care which one? Which one do you have access to? And does your access include the ability to screen by changes in rating? Are they looking for just a few companies? Or do they need all changes in a certain time period?

Generally for these kinds of finance questions, I'll start hunting around for a library guide or some other kinds of clues that may help me figure out where to start my real search. A Google search for *bond ratings changes* brought me to this industry association site that has some good explanations: www.investinginbonds .com/learnmore.asp?catid = 7&subcatid = 72&id = 53. It does mention that when one of the rating agencies is going to downgrade, they'll have a press release. I might follow that up by looking for the ratings part of the agencies and see if they make these announcements easy to find and/or do some kind of article search. Depending on what your patron needs, this may or may not do the trick. If they need to generate a list of any company that has had a change (up or down) in a specific window of time, that's probably going to require some kind of more hardcore financial database.

Some more digging (googling, really) by adding the word *screen* to my above search brought me to a Bloomberg help page from Princeton that mentions that Bloomberg has a Company Credit Rating Revisions Monitor that looks like it would track and screen for changes in ratings. But of course, you'd have to have a Bloomberg terminal. I'm sure there are some similar tools in some of the other financial databases (most of which are beyond the scope of this book).

When all else fails, I turn to colleagues who are more informed about these kinds of topics. In the last part of the book I mention the BusLib e-mail group. For this kind of question, I might search around in their archives to see if there are any clues (I just did that . . . didn't see anything, unfortunately, for changes). If not, send out a call for help on the list. Luckily, here in my library we also have a separate department that deals a lot with raw data pools and giant screening projects like this, so I'd probably run this by them, too.

Q: I had a student who was looking for historical (i.e., at least for the past twenty years) analyst forecasts for the S&P 500. Bloomberg goes back to 2006 and is nice and neat and exportable into Excel. He also wants historical quotes for the past twenty years for the S&P 500 so he can compare the forecasts to the actual results.

I talked to the Bloomberg reps last week and they only have data to 2006 (they aren't known for historical data), and I can't seem to find it in SDC or Datastream.

A: Yes, Bloomberg is never very helpful when it comes to bulk historical data.

For this question one of the things I'd want to clarify is whether it matters what source the forecasts are coming from. It sounds like you found the Bloomberg forecasts, but if I understand it correctly, those forecasts come directly from

Bloomberg analysts. Similar firms have their own forecasts (with varying rates of accuracy). It can be tricky to find historical forecasts because often whoever made them doesn't want them floating around for anyone to look at later and say, "Boy, were they off."

Getting historical quotes for the S&P 500 shouldn't be as difficult, but again you'll need some clarification—does the patron want quotes for the index overall (I'm assuming he doesn't care about individual constituents)? And for what time frame? Annual, daily, quarterly? Yahoo! Finance and other free sites cover index prices, and many of the fee-based financial data resources (like Compustat and CRSP) should have this as well.

I'm not sure yet about the historical forecasts, but I think you're on the right track in looking at places like SDC or Datastream. I might troll the BusLib archives on this one or send out a call for help to see if anyone else has come across this. Another thing you could do would be to look for papers on this topic and see what kinds of sources were used. This seems like something that would be written about in the academic literature.

Q: I recently had a question where a student wanted to find current and historical prices for cattle in Spain. This was difficult for many reasons, and I spent several hours researching. In the process I learned a great deal about imports and exports and the market in Spain. I found several sources and websites, but never managed to find what we really wanted to find.

A: Well, it sounds like you did the right thing to start—begin digging around and see where the clues lead you. My one suggestion would be to step back even further from the specific question at hand (two pieces—cattle prices and Spain) and see if you can identify the broader categories they fit into (in this case, commodities and Europe). Also, sometimes you can add the word *data* to see if you get pointed toward data resources.

Sometimes, especially in a Google search or other search, being too specific can narrow your options. Again, ask yourself who cares about this information and see if that can help lead you to a more acceptable answer.

Broadening out to larger categories won't necessarily give you better answers, but it's another search strategy to try.

Finally, if your search doesn't pan out, try to identify who might know this kind of thing. Call a finance professor at your college or a nearby university. Use the BusLib e-mail list to see if anyone has dealt with this before. These kinds of advanced financial business reference questions can be daunting, but don't feel like you have to be the expert here.

Q: I asked one librarian about questions that can be challenging, and he mentioned getting information on hedge funds, especially those that are guarded.

A: I never know what to do with hedge funds, either. Apparently, they are not as required as some other financial instruments to report their information. (Although recent banking legislation like the Dodd Frank Act have changed some of this: http://en.wikipedia.org/wiki/Hedge_fund#Regulation.)

A lot of times when I'm faced with more advanced financial analysis questions, I see if there is a library guide out there that will help give me a clue or two. I did a Google search for *hedge funds library guide site:.edu* and found a Harvard Baker Library guide to Hedge Funds: www.library.hbs.edu/guides/hedgefunds.html. If nothing else, this would give you a few places to turn to (or to know that you don't subscribe to some of the more high-end tools, if that's the case).

Q: Finding information on copper prices in the 1960s is a real challenge.

A: I think finding commodity prices in general can be pretty daunting, let alone historical prices (sometimes it's hard just to remember that things like copper and other metals are considered commodities and to use that terminology to help in the searching).

If nothing else, they definitely lean toward a "beyond Biz Ref 101" difficulty level. One thing I do when faced with commodities questions is see if I can identify a research guide that will give me some starting points or other clues. Often I start with the Harvard Baker Library guides, since I figure they'll cover just about everything (not that I'll have access to it). In this case, I didn't see commodities in their list of research guides, but they also have a handy list of databases by subject—and one of the subjects is commodities. Here's their list: www.library.hbs.edu/databases/by_subject/commodities.html. Most of these databases are going to be seen only at large, academic institutions with a big business or econ program, but it doesn't hurt to look so that you can at least identify some potential sources and see if you can help your patron follow up on those. (FYI, I would use Global Financial Data if you have access to it. They're very good on coverage of historical prices.)

Additionally, if I'm still looking for more clues, I'd google terms like *historical copper prices* or *historical metal prices*. I'd probably start to see things like the London Metal Exchange and might be able to add that to my bag of clues (and maybe even stumble across the answer).

Again, try to focus on finding a source for the data, rather than the data itself. It's easy to start spinning your wheels online wondering why you can't find historical copper prices for free, when it just might be the case that the information you're looking for is only going to be in one or two fee-based places.

Q: (1) Provide examples of foreign direct investment that have occurred within the last ten years. (2) Provide an example of a company that has entered a foreign market for the first time within the last ten years. What methods did they use to gain entry into the foreign market?

A: These are stumpers that make me think there are probably some good academic guides out there that would provide some clues. I did a quick Google search of *fdi site:.edu library* (*FDI* is commonly used as the abbreviation for *foreign direct investment*, but you could try both). I was immediately pointed to sites from Yale and Harvard, both of which provided a lot of resources on doing research on FDI and emerging markets (another term you can now use). Since you need examples, too, you can continue with a literature search in articles on FDI and case studies or examples; see what turns up and tweak your search accordingly. Also, there are probably trade journals that cover this topic specifically that you could also try to identify (if they're not already pulled out on the academic guides).

Q: Patrons want to know what significance the P/E ratio has when evaluating a company and how to use it when comparing companies.

A: This is a question that you can use not only to teach yourself, but also to point your patron toward some useful resources, about what P/E is and other measures of comparing companies. With this kind of question, if you're being thrown for a loop right from the start (e.g., you're not even sure what P/E stands for), a great place to start is in one of the business dictionaries. Investopedia has some great explanations and tools, and the Campbell R. Harvey's Hypertextual Finance Glossary would give you even more technical info.

Q: Should I invest in (a particular company)? My patrons often come to me for advice I'm obviously unqualified to give—I'd like to be able to confidently point them to the necessary tools and resources for them to make their decisions.

A: Good question! I want to know, too! My colleagues and I always used to joke that we should be rich, given all the access to business databases and other financial info that we had. But, much as we'd like it, there's no secret formula to getting rich quick through investing—or any other way, regardless of what those late-night infomercials might tell us. You have the right attitude: just as you wouldn't diagnose a medical condition or offer tax advice or write someone's history paper, you don't want to start voicing your own opinion and giving business advice. You can tell patrons that you're there to point them to the resources and get them started, and they should be happy with that. You'll find that some patrons need a little more handholding, but in that case, just get them set up to begin some research on their own and then make sure they feel comfortable returning to you if they have questions later. That's really all you can do. But if you do have a good tip on a great company, do tell the rest of us!

Q: I need the 2007 and 2008 EBITDA for NewsCorp's filmed entertainment division. The virtual reference patron who inquired was not part of my university community and had access only to free resources.

A: This question seems like it might be straightforward until you break it down. First, you want to know what EBITDA is (some finance glossaries and other resources are pointed to in chapter 6, "Investment Research"). FYI, it's *earnings before interest, taxes, depreciation, and amortization*. But you all knew that, right? (Honestly, I know what the acronym stands for, but that's about it!). Then, the real stumper is going to be, does NewsCorp break out financials for their "filmed entertainment division"? And, if so, does it break it out to the EBITDA level? Plus, the fiscal year 2008 is probably not over yet for most companies [at the time of this question], so the patron may need to rethink the years they're asking for. On top of all that, you need free resources. Well, if NewsCorp doesn't break out that division, even a fee-based resource won't help. I'd point this patron to company filings from NewsCorp and tell them they'll need to dig. EBITDA is not necessarily reported, so they may need to find the individual data points and do the math, too. I think the most help you can provide the patron in this situation is the clue to first figure out if NewsCorp provides financials broken out by division. If not, they may need to figure out a different plan. Ask them what they need the number for, too . . . would other profitability information help? Would looking at other companies that primarily work in "filmed entertainment" EBITDAs work? Maybe a literature search would provide some info. Or an analyst report.

Q: I'm working the reference desk today and the new Value Line just arrived. I don't know if this is a stumper or not, but I have no idea what to do with Value Line. When people have asked me for it, I've prayed that they knew what they were doing with it. Help, anyone? Maybe an overview or something?

A: Value Line has confused many a poor librarian—you're not alone. Not only does it contain a lot of complicated investment data, it's also kind of confusing in how it's updated and filed! Usually you get two Value Line "thingies" per week: an index and a new issue. Issues are updated on a rolling basis, so when you get a new edition 2 you go to the binder (or folder system) and take out the old edition 2 and put in the new edition 2, as well as replacing the old index with the new index. (What you do with the old editions and indexes varies by library—most end up throwing them away [because they get converted to microfilm].) Each edition focuses on a few industries, and these stay the same across editions. For example, chemical companies are always in edition 8. Companies in the same industry are grouped together. You can use the index to look up which edition your company is in—you'll have to know the page range each edition covers (which also stays the same). The reason people want to use Value Line is because they rate stocks and industries on a special proprietary investment formula and basically try to predict which ones will be the best ones to invest in. (Remember—as reference librarians we can refer patrons to these kinds of tools, but we're not in the business of suggesting stock purchases or portfolio management. That said, we can still try to explain how this thing works.)

At the front of each index, each of the industries is ranked based on the stock performance of the companies within that industry. At the front of each edition, you can see individual companies (depending on the industry covered in that edition) pulled out and ranked according to various factors such as "timeliness" (how well a stock will do in the next twelve months), safety (how safe an investment a stock is), beta (how sensitive a stock is to market fluctuations), and other components. You can go to the Value Line page for each company to get a full profile, which is basically a snapshot of how it is doing and how Value Line predicts it will do. Value Line only covers public companies, and I haven't gotten into Small Cap versus Large Cap (there are actually two indexes and two editions coming in to your library if you get the full set—Large Cap tends to have larger companies like Walmart and the Small Cap, well, smaller companies. If your patron can't find their company in one index, make sure they try the other).

I also haven't gotten into their other products like Selection and Opinion and a few others. This page points to a number of Value Line guides, including The Complete Overview of the Value Line Investment Survey: www3.valueline.com/sup_howtoinvest.aspx. Also, here is a link from the Value Line site on how to read a Value Line page: www.valueline.com/Tools/How_To_Use_Value_Line_Pages.aspx. This can be a really useful tool—I believe there is a print version available, and at the previous library where I worked, we had copies printed out that we gave to patrons who were new to Value Line (mostly students who were told by their professor to use it—actual small investors usually seem to know their way around Value Line . . . you might want to hit one up for some tips—really!).

One thing I can suggest is to pick a company and look it up in Value Line—see what you can find and what other information you find around it. Often using these tools is the best way to start to get an understanding of what's in them.

STUMPERS:
DEMOGRAPHICS AND CONSUMER BEHAVIOR

Q: A small niche magazine owner wants to expand nationally via franchising. He wants data to show investors that there are some/many good potential markets for his publication in the United States.

He wants to target markets that have the following criteria:

■ Smaller "tier 3" cities and/or clusters of towns with total house-holds in each of 10,000 to 30,000
■ Median household income of $75,000-plus
■ Highly educated population

I'm stumped. Where should I start?

A: American FactFinder from the U.S. Census should have the ability to screen for most of these. It won't necessarily be straightforward in terms of running the search, but if he digs around in there, he's likely to find quite a bit of data. The trick will be to get it cross-tabulated, meaning, for example, of the cities with X number of $75,000 household incomes, what percentage of those are highly educated? You may be able to find each separate criteria, but it's when you want to combine things that demographics get trickier.

He could also explore what's available through ReferenceUSA—they actually have a number of products that cover consumers (not just a company directory) that might be of use. After meeting with one of their reps recently I learned that they often work directly with companies to run large data pulls for them to generate e-mail target lists and the like. So that might be an option, too, since it sounds like this particular patron could not only use this kind of info for his business as it exists now but also to provide good data for potential investors. Of course, this option would cost some money up front, but it might be a good investment if this is something the entrepreneur wants to investigate.

Q: Most of the business questions I get are from entrepreneurs working on a business plan or just trying to see how viable their idea for a new business is. Sometimes it's especially hard to help people with unique ideas. The following questions are from a person working on an interior decorating business based entirely online: "I am starting an online interior decorating business. Where can I find free industry information? How can I find my target customer?"

A: One thing that might help both you and your patron as you dive into this kind of research is emphasizing to her right from the start that it will be a process and that you'll likely have to break things out into steps. In other words, it will take time and perseverance—and no, you do not have the secret book *Top 10 Never-Fail Steps to Starting Your Multimillion-Dollar Online Interior Decorating Business* hiding behind the counter.

Start with the industry and see what you can find. Look for associations and trade publications. Maybe even look for some general online business books. Don't forget to show them some of the many small business resources—the SBA site and business plan templates, etc.

For target customers, that's going to be trickier. You can help the patron look for articles on consumers and interior decorating as well as consumers and online target markets. Since they are planning on doing something based entirely online, they won't necessarily have to worry about geographic specificity, but there will be other things they'll need to consider that some of those general "how to start an online business" books might cover. And then they may find that there are even more steps—building a website, generating traffic to it, marketing it, etc. There are likely companies out there that specialize in helping business startups with some of these questions, but if they want to do it all themself, they'll have to pay with a lot of time and possibly trial and error.

Q: A patron wants to know about all purchases made over the past five years with a breakdown of where the purchases were being made. He also wanted to find information on how many items are returned from online purchases.

A: Hoo-boy. What this patron really wants is proprietary and, if available at all, very expensive data. Most of the sources available will only cover people's overall habits and some data. But getting down to sales by retailer, and online sales at that (retailers aren't required to break out their online sales), will be hard, and my instinct is that getting the returns data near to impossible (not to mention getting all this for five years).

That said, there is a database called eMarketer that covers a lot of online retail and consumer behavior topics. That might be a place where you could find some numbers. Another big name in this area is a company called Forrester. You can also look at major retail resources, too, like the NRF (National Retail Federation) and some related publications (like *Stores* magazine) for general data on retail sales that may be broken into online numbers (but again, probably not by specific retailer).

I'd also do an article search to see if you could find any reports on online shopping and returns behavior—if you're lucky, a data source will be cited. If nothing else, you might get an estimate about online sales and returns. Keep in mind different terminology to try—*e-commerce* is still frequently used, and the U.S. government even uses *electronic shopping* sometimes, I noticed.

You might also want to help the patron look into product returns processes/ practices for online sales in general. It looks like different retailers have different practices. (Some allow in-store returns, for example. Others pay for shipping. Other retailers are online-only, so they either have to partner with someone that has a physical presence or come up with some other options.)

You can also look for articles just on product returns to see what kinds of info starts turning up from there. You might be able to find enough data where you could do some math to subtract total retail sales and product returns and compare to online sales, but it won't be straightforward.

Q: These kinds of questions stump me: "How much do people spend on swimsuits?" or "I need psychographic information about shoes." I usually let patrons know that in marketing, it is difficult to get actual hard numbers since companies don't want to share this kind of information with their competitors. I try to help them narrow down their queries by age group, location, company, etc. I show them U.S. Census data, New Strategist publications, and sometimes Business and Company Resource Center or Gale (which we don't have access to at my library, but the public library down the street does). How can I help them find the specific information that they are looking for? Especially the psychographics?

A: Ah, psychographics: trying to get into the mind of the consumer. The suggestions you're giving your patrons are exactly what I suggest. When you're trying to delve into the psychology of shopping, point them to articles—try adding terms like *attitudes or psychology* and steer away (for the most part) from the term *psychographics* itself. Paco Underhill is considered one of the gurus in this area. He wrote *Why We Buy: The Science of Shopping* (Simon and Schuster, 2008, rev. ed.) and now has a consulting firm in this area (www.envirosell.com/index .php?option=com_content&task=view&id=28&Itemid=135).

This is yet another area where there are no easy answers, and also yet another area where brainstorming with the patron can bring up all kinds of options— maybe you can find some more general articles on the shopping habits of men or women and extrapolate from there. Or maybe the search will be for *fashion and shopping and psychology* and turn up some leads. Assure the patron that finding information will involve a process and that he won't necessarily find an article that covers exactly what he's looking for, but that this is OK. Often students and other patrons are not comfortable making those logical connections and extrapolations from what they find, so this is something else to be aware of.

Q: I received an e-mail question recently where the person was looking for sales trends of men's and women's underwear in the United States in the past few years, as well as for specific companies: Target, Walmart, Victoria's Secret, Kmart. I was able to find some background information on the underwear industry but could not find specific numbers.

A: You'll be glad to know that in this case, it's not you, it's the specificity of this question. Everyone (well, everyone in the underwear industry, anyway) would like to know how much of it is sold, what kinds and where and for how much. This is really detailed internal company information. In the intro parts of the book we'll talk about how some questions just can't be answered and how you'll want to step back and ask yourself, "Would a company want their competitors to know this info?"

That said, there is still useful info to be had out there. You did what I would do—give the patron some background info on the industry. You might find some ballpark total industry size numbers as well as perhaps an industry association or something like that. Keep in mind that this industry might be hard to define. What do they mean by "underwear"? Are they including lingerie? Are they including long underwear and things like that? Also, you may have found that for some industries, like this one, reports will package more than one area together—in this case, you'll often find underwear and hosiery together. Often, you'll have to take whatever you can get.

On the off chance that you can find some store-specific info, you can try some article searching and see if anything has been written—you might be able to find something that provides a clue, like "according to the underwear association, major retailers like Target and Walmart account for X percent of total industry sales." But be prepared for a lot of digging. Similarly, you can look into some of the specialty companies like Victoria's Secret and see if they give some industry data, too (although you'll find that Victoria's Secret is a subsidiary of a larger company that also owns Bath and Body Works and Pink and other stores, so the data might not be broken out).

Q: Our community college serves a large geographic area that includes many small towns and rural areas. We sometimes get questions from people wanting to start a business, and they want to know how to get information about the potential customers in a particular area. Most of the towns around here are too small to have been part of market research, and patrons aren't always able to get the info they need from the county-level data available.

A: The census might have some top-level info on community areas. They have something called American FactFinder that, once you figure it out, can pull lots of different kinds of statistical and demographic data. They also have a "Quick Facts" feature if you just need some top-level info. If you just need a quick population count, try their population finder.

Remember, one of the trickiest things when it comes to finding demographic data related to a particular geographic area is that often the data is broken out only in certain ways (and not necessarily the way your patron is looking for). For example, he wants a specific neighborhood, but data is only pulled by zip code or by county. So be aware of that. Also, all the data he wants may not be included—only certain age groups, certain income ranges, etc., may be covered. And it's very difficult to find out religious background by geographic area. It's commonly asked for, but since it's not included on the census questionnaire, you're not going to find it there.

Another tip, if you live in a larger urban area, is to try to identify whether or not there is a local group that tracks statistics. For example, in Chicago there is something called the Metro Chicago Information Center, with all kinds of data related to the city and surrounding suburbs. Much easier to use than the census.

And look beyond the census, too. Do some article searching and think creatively. Ask yourself who cares about this kind of information and see if you can drill down from the top.

Q: This semester, a patron asked, "I need to find out: how many women in the United States between the ages of 25–35, 35–45, 45–55, live in Chicago, LA, Austin, NY, and Seattle, and report a household income of more than $100,000?"

A: This does seem like it would be reported somewhere, doesn't it? The trick will be getting the breakouts the way she's asking. It's not necessarily the case that the ages will be in ten-year increments or that $100,000 is the top level of income.

The other trick is that you need to find it for women reporting this income level. The census focuses on households and doesn't necessarily cross-tabulate to show women and income levels or men and income levels. On some level, this question kind of needs to be clarified—women reporting a household income of any amount isn't really trackable. Does she mean households with incomes over $100,000 that have women in those age groups in them? Again, it will be tricky to get the data broken down into the age brackets, but if nothing else, you could find out the total number of households in those cities with that income and the number of women in those (approximate) age ranges in those cities.

As with some of these other stumpers, I'd start to look for sources of data rather than the answer. Try searching for *women and incomes and United States* to see if there are studies out there (there must be), and then cross your fingers that they cover the cities you're looking at. Alternatively, you may need to look at each city individually and see if there are any specific studies. You may be able to find groups that focus on women and incomes and go from there.

Q: How much ketchup was sold in 2008 within the 76019 zip code?

A: What, you don't have the 2010 edition of the "North American ketchup/catsup sales by brand, price, and zip code"?

The more granular you get with these kinds of questions, the more difficult it will be to find an answer. When it comes to particular kinds of products and how many have been sold where, sometimes you'll have to make do with some total numbers and then extrapolate. For example, you might be able to find total 2008 ketchup sales for the United States (or maybe even by state) by doing an article or online search. You then might be able to find some total 2008 U.S. population numbers to get an estimate of how much ketchup per person is consumed. (Or bought, at least—that might be something to clarify with the patron. Is he looking for sales figures or amounts of ketchup sold?) You could then try to get some population numbers for the 76019 zip code and see what you can come up with.

Don't forget to try to identify ketchup and/or condiments associations or other groups who care about this topic.

All this is not to say you can't find entire reports on ketchup—or, more likely, ketchup and mustard and mayo. I did a quick online search and found the table of contents for a 2006 report on the "sandwich spread" market, which does contain some top-level numbers (www.packagedfacts.com/sitemap/product .asp?productid=1209575). But chances of getting that broken down by zip code are slim (so don't worry, it's not you, it's the nature of these kinds of questions).

Q: For a business class, can one group of students strategically locate a hypothetical company (paintball equipment) in a defined geographic area based upon known demographic data on those who are paintball fanatics? In the past we have had some luck "locating a business" using census data or the MOSAIC info out of DemographicsNow, but finding out info on the paintball industry has flopped, and attempting to understand the demographic hasn't worked well either.

A: Oh, my . . . this one is a stumper on a few levels. First, the paintball industry is going to be hard to define. It's made up of lots of small, private companies. Second, last time I checked, paintball fanaticism was not covered in the census. Anytime you try to get demographic data on a small, very targeted group where you're very rigid with your definition, you're going to have trouble. In this case, I'd allow yourself some leeway and let yourself (with the help of the students) brainstorm on paintball fanatics—what else do they like? Can you start to find data on these hobbies and then, through the transitive property, apply it to paintball people? That said, there's probably at least one or two local, national, or international paintball associations out there. Don't forget to look for them for guidance and potentially some data. Also, keep in mind that this is for a class and that the professor knows (or should) that this kind of specific data is not likely to be readily available, if it's available at all. Often, the goal of an assignment like this is to get the students to think about the topic and apply what they've been learning. Often it's OK to make some leaps of logic when you're building an industry and demographic profile as long as you can back up your thought process. If this is not the case and the students are insistent that their professor needs real data or they will fail, maybe check in with the professor on the assignment and see what can be done as an acceptable compromise.

STUMPERS: STATISTICS

Q: A student came to the reference desk and asked, "How do I calculate the inflation rate for the past ten years? My professor told me I must use an official government source to find this."

A: In Google's advanced search, you can limit to just .gov results. A quick search for *inflation* limited to .gov sites pointed me to the Consumer Price Index page (www.bls.gov/cpi/). Digging around here you'll find some explanations as well as some historical data (going back to 1913). Alternatively, you can search around for sites related to inflation rates and check the sources of their data. A quick search this way indicated that most were using CPI data.

When in doubt, when it comes to government/economic statistics, I'll often start at the Census.gov page and use their A-to-Z index. In this case, their entry "Inflation" points you to the Bureau of Labor Statistics page (which is where the CPI data comes from).

Alternatively, there is USA.gov. It limits to .gov automatically, so it's essentially the same as the search strategy just mentioned, but letting students know there's a separate site sometimes makes it "click" for them a little more easily than telling them to limit to .gov, if that makes sense.

Q: I am trying to research a NAICS number and the growth it has had in the last five to seven years consecutively. The number is NAICS 541611. I have searched www.census.gov, and the most recent numbers come from the 2002 census. I have searched www.commerce.gov, and it takes me to census.gov. After an exhaustive search I found some figures at the U.S. Bureau of Labor Statistics, but only as recent as 2008. I'm sure there are more recent figures out there but I was unable to discover them.

A: This is a tricky one. One thing I would do before diving in to find the updated NAICS counts is to talk to the patron about what they're trying to do with the data. They may be hung up on NAICS codes but not understand some of their limitations. I see that this particular code refers to "Administrative and Consulting Services."

You may be able to point the person to some other resources that would cover this industry beyond a code count. Keep in mind, one of the major drawbacks (in my opinion, anyway) of industry codes is that companies can do more than one thing, and one code won't capture this. For example, I'm wondering if a company like IBM gets included in the count for "Administrative and Consulting Services." It's my understanding that they have a pretty big consulting arm, but that's not the first thing you think of when it comes to IBM.

As for the dates on the data, the economic census is done only every five years, so there will be limits on how current the data you get from it will be.

Q: How do I find the latest information on the gross national product of the United States?

A: Since I didn't know this one off the top of my head, I started with some quick Google searches. I'm expecting to find a clue to point me to which government agency tracks this number.

What I found was a site telling me that *GDP* is actually the preferred term, so when I searched for that, I was pointed to the Bureau of Economic Analysis, where I found a news release for the GDP with a recent date. I looked at this and then went to the main BEA site and searched for *GDP* and was pointed to their main section on GDP.

If you need additional GDP data, I can recommend a database called Global Financial Data—it's a subscription site (i.e., fee-based), but if you're at an academic library with a big business program, you might have it. You can also search it for free to see what they do have: www.globalfinancialdata.com. GDP is one of their main data series types.

And, just for kicks, I did a Google search for *GDP historical* and was pointed to this site: http://eh.net/hmit/gdp/. It seems fairly reputable and will pull GDP data by year, along with some other data points like population. This also made me remember that the Statistical Abstract of the United States would be a useful source for this kind of data, as would some of the databases that cover international data.

STUMPERS: **INTERNATIONAL**

Q: How many municipal water and/or wastewater treatment plants have been owned by foreign corporations for the past ten years? Names of those companies?

A: This one had me wincing from stumper pain at first glance, too. No quick and easy answer off the bat, but this is yet another situation where asking yourself

"Who cares?" can help. A quick Google search for *municipal water treatment plants* points toward an EPA site (http://cfpub.epa.gov/npdes/home.cfm?program_id = 13). I'm thinking that regardless of which municipality you're dealing with, they all have to deal with EPA regulation of some kind. It's possible that there are some numbers here to contact where you could find someone who could explain ownership. That would be a start, anyway, and then the trick would be to find some way to screen across multiple plants and back ten years. But baby steps first.

It also looks like there are some international/national/state-level water quality associations that might have some info.

I'd also maybe identify some local area water treatment plants and again get on the phone to see if someone there can explain the ownership set up. And, of course, don't forget that you might find a trove of clues in an article search—try searching for *water treatment plants and ownership* or similar combinations and be careful not to get bogged down in the foreign/ten years part at first. You could also see if you can find anything in articles related to foreign ownership or similar trends. From a quick search, it looks like most municipal plants are owned either by the town or the county (although legal disputes sometimes arise over ownership).

One thing that you might find with a question like this is that the landscape is too varied to get this info consistently across all municipalities, so you might have to work with the patron to narrow down the range of plants that he is interested in and start smaller, rather than looking at all water treatment plants.

Q: I had a question from a graduate student wanting to know what the major imports/exports are between the United States and EAC (East African Community). I directed him to www.ustr.gov for the information. He then wanted to know who the specific manufacturers are for the major exports from the EAC. I didn't know where to go from there.

A: You did the right thing by heading to a government site for trade data to start (there's also http://trade.gov, which is probably pointed to somewhere on the www.ustr.gov site, as well as Export.gov). There's also export and import data on a site called NationMaster.com. Keep in mind that many of the international databases will also likely include some economic data, including export figures (but not necessarily down to the level of commodity).

One thing that might need to get clarified is whether or not EAC is a commonly used category and if the data sources you're finding use it. It's possible that the patron would have to come up with a list of specific countries that make up the EAC and go in country by country and then do some calculations. With a quick Google search for *EAC*, I also found this website: www.eac.int, which might also have some data the patron could use.

Once you have some of the trade number totals, determining who the actual manufacturers are will be a little trickier. Sounds like you'll first have to determine what those major exports from the EAC are and then use some kind of directory type of database (like OneSource or Orbis) and then screen by types of export and country.

There's always article searching, too, which you could do on the general topic of Africa and exports. You could get a general sense of top exports and largest exporting countries and then start to look around for specific companies.

Q: How do you find information on what the exchange rate was on a particular date? If your patron needs that information in U.S. dollars, would you need to find the exchange rate for the date the report was published and then work from there?

A: That would be an example of an international question combining a bit with a historical financial question to make it that much trickier. These are exactly the kinds of things you'll want to be on the lookout for whenever you're dealing with numbers and business reference of any kind.

Luckily, a quick Google search for *historical exchange rates* pulls up some (seemingly) reputable sources. Since exchange rates can change daily, this can be a hard thing to track in a print source (unless you're getting annual averages).

And, at least until recently, you can check back issues of large newspapers to find some global exchange rates. Also, Global Financial Database covers historical exchange rates, so if you needed to track a number of currencies or export a lot of years' worth of data, going to a fee-based product might be worth it.

As for doing the actual currency conversion, I would point your patron to the resources and let them decide whether or not they need to adjust her figures.

Q: One of my staff who was working on her degree in business had this problem: She was doing a paper for her econ class. She had to research the principle imports and exports of a country. In her case it was Australia. The problem was that she could find information only on categories of goods as opposed to the individual goods. We ended up using the *CIA World Factbook*. Is there anything that would have been more useful?

A: In this case my first thought was to hit the International Trade Administration (you'd be pointed to this in a Google search for trade statistics or something similar). Also, when in doubt, you can start at the census page and use their index—they point to a ton of resources. OFFSTATS (www.offstats.auckland.ac.nz) would be another good resource. The problem with trade data (and other kinds of data) is that it's not always broken out to the level that you like. Trade statistics are so confusing anyway, if you don't deal with them a lot. What I've always done is to dig through a couple of these sources (and I think the *CIA World Factbook* is a good start, but probably not as deep as you can get), look for clues, and then finally try to identify someone either at the International Trade Administration or another trade organization to ask questions or identify an association of whatever good I'm researching and see if they can provide any additional input. Also, when you're looking for a specific exports of a specific country, you can limit yourself too much by being too detailed in your searching by putting in too many keywords. In a case like this, you might be better off just looking for *exports and Australia* and drilling down in whatever resources you might find, rather than trying to find the exact data right off the bat. I would also suggest investigating Australia government resources that may be online. Australia may have a department similar to the U.S. Department of Commerce with this type of import and export information (and in this case, it would be in English). For example, using the Australian Trade Commission website at www.austrade.com/Home1513/default .aspx, click on the "Australian Industry Expertise" tab and you will find links to more information on broad industries that export. Digging further will take you to more links that might lead to the level of stats that your employee was looking for. It's easy to get "U.S.-centric" even when dealing with international business research, so looking to the country in question is always a good idea.

Q: What was the financial surplus of Malaysia since 2003?

A: This sounds like an international economics kind of question to me. Look through resources like the IMF and World Bank and see what you can find for Malaysia in general. You can also search for articles on *Malaysia and economy* to see what comes up, but those are unlikely to give you the exact numbers (although they may point you toward a source).

A quick online search for *Malaysia economic data* turned up a Department of Statistics Malaysia (www.statistics.gov.my/portal/index.php?lang=en), but on quick glance, their data doesn't go back that far. That same Google search also pulled up the NationMaster listing for Malaysia (www.nationmaster.com/country/my-malaysia/eco-economy). Digging through here might point you toward a source (or the data itself). Also, a search in Google Scholar for papers on this topic might also provide some clues to where the data is hiding (and also whether *financial surplus* is the correct term to search).

Q: I recently had someone who was looking for information about creating trademarks for a small business. He also wanted to know about trademark protection on products sold overseas. The question was tough because he wanted very general information and didn't want to look at specific countries. These were some of the questions he asked: "Are registered trademarks recognized overseas? Do you have a listing of countries that recognize U.S. trademarks? How long does trademark protection typically last in other countries? How much does international protection of trademarks typically cost?"

A: In this case I would start with the go-to resource for trademark information which, as far as I know, is the U.S. Patent and Trademark Office. This site would at least be a good starting point and contains some of the basics (although maybe not with the international scope that this patron was looking for). I searched across the PTO site for the word *international* and did see a mention of another office called PCT Legal Administration. Apparently there is something called the Patent Cooperation Treaty. This sounds like something to follow up on.

With these kinds of stumpers I definitely focus on looking for sources of information rather than the answer itself. At the end of the day, what this patron really might need is an attorney specializing in international trademark to get to the bottom of his question.

Q: A patron wanted to know: for companies owned/based in GCC countries, what are the percentages of women working in them? He really wanted to know what the numbers are for local women working in them (women who hold a passport of a GCC country), but it didn't matter—I couldn't find anything. I finally got something from the *Economist*, but it was rather general and a few years old.

A: This one is definitely going to be tricky. First, you'll need to clarify *GCC countries*. Does he mean Gulf Cooperation Council? What countries are those? Then, the next thing to do is not get hung up on the GCC country piece of the equation. Ask yourself, could I find this information for any country? The United States? Also, how do I identify companies based in these countries? Those would be the first steps.

I think what you'd quickly realize is that this isn't necessarily readily available info. Companies don't generally break down their employee numbers by gender. You can often find total number of employees, but then you'd have to hit upon a special study, perhaps, or try to find some other clues to get the male/female breakdown. Perhaps if you could come up with a list of companies in each country—get a count of companies as well as an employee count (and I'm not saying that would be totally easy, but it would be a more likely starting point), then perhaps find an article or something that reports on female employment rates in the countries in question. You'd want to search broadly here, too—*females or women and employment or working and Middle East or Bahrain or GCC*, etc. It is not likely going to be totally scientific or exact, but with some digging, you may be able to come up with some creative estimates.

Q: Does Chile have a dominant, domestic auto manufacturer? It wasn't too difficult to learn about auto manufacturing in Chile, but the information tended to focus on major auto manufacturers based in foreign countries, not on auto manufacturers based in Chile.

A: If the patron was trying to identify a major company that is based in Chile, then your approach would maybe have to involve using some kind of business directory where you screened for auto manufacturers and Chile as a location. I did a quick search like this in a database called OneSource where I selected "Chile" and searched for the auto and truck manufacturers industry category. It pulled up seventy-one companies. When I sorted by sales, I saw companies like GM Chile and other major U.S. and foreign auto player subsidiaries, plus what seemed to be bus and other larger vehicle manufacturers. You could work with the patron to see if this was getting closer to what they were looking for. You may need to ask them for more information to determine what they really want to know. Maybe they want to know the number one consumer auto brand driven in Chile—that would be a different kind of question. As you can see, a lot of times, these questions (and the answers) are often not very straightforward, so be prepared for some creative approaches, and partner with the patron to get them to clarify what they're really trying to find.

Q: What permits do I need to export grains to Bangladesh?

A: That's a good question. I'd start by looking into sources of info for exporting in general. A quick search will bring up the Export.gov site, and they have surprisingly easy-to-find contact information and more. You can call them, and they even offer contact info for their international offices, including one in India (http://export .gov/india/). It says in the first half of this page, "The U.S. Commercial Service of the U.S. Embassy helps U.S. firms export goods and services to India."

Additionally, you could follow up on the "grain" part of the equation to see what leads it might provide. A quick search in Google for *exporting grains* brought up the North American Export Grain Association (www.naega.org). This might be another good resource.

These are the kinds of places where I would be directing the patron, rather than trying to determine on my own what the permit requirements were. That sounds like it's veering into legal advice and beyond, which you'd want to avoid.

Q: Our MBA capstone project is to research a particular business or industry in a developed and developing nation (e.g., U.K. and Dominica) with an eye to opening a business in those nations. I have trouble finding information for some of the smaller developing countries. Database sources have much more for larger countries like the United Kingdom. The resources needed often vary widely with the type of business students are looking into (opening a movie theater, say).

A: One term that is used for these kinds of countries is *emerging markets*, and a related concept is *foreign direct investment*. You could try to identify some key resources in these areas to see if they provide additional information. But one reason you're not finding as much data is because those markets are developing. When you combine that with trying to find info on a specific market (especially ones like movie theaters), it gets even harder. Look for anything you can find on business start-ups in those developing countries—you may get pointed to some organizations or other groups that can point you toward more. And don't forget to try some general resources on country information to see what you can find. Sometimes a search for *doing business in* and the name of the country in question can point to some useful information, too. Also, look for local government resources—most countries want to attract businesses and may have set up sites to assist in the process.

Q: A student recently asked for articles about the "global marketing of the Palm Pixi." This might not be that difficult of a question to answer, but I wasn't sure how to answer it.

I also wasn't sure what was meant by *global marketing*. This was a question that came in via e-mail (as most of our questions do, since our students are all distance-learning students), and I never heard back from the student when I tried to get clarification. Maybe this is common lingo in the business world and I just don't know what it means.

A: What? You couldn't find the hundred-page internal report from HP detailing their plans for world domination by their Palm Pixi product, including spending by country?

This is one of those questions that gets more difficult the more granular you get. The student wants info on a specific product, the Palm Pixi. As I've suggested for other stumpers, step back from this one and start broadly. First—what is a Palm Pixi? A quick Google search will show you that it's a kind of smartphone/mobile phone/telecommunication device. A little more digging on Palm and you'll find that they're a unit of HP. Now you've got something to work with. You can find some company profiles of HP and see if any mention is made of their Palm division and, ideally, Palm Pixi. But maybe you won't find this level of detail. That's OK. Keep in mind that companies aren't required to tell you about their marketing plans, global or otherwise, so you have to do some sleuthing.

I wouldn't worry about the "global" part of this and instead focus on the main concept of marketing. Maybe you'll find an article about HP's plan to launch Palm products (maybe not the Pixi) in Europe or Asia that's related. Maybe you can glean some info on their approach by digging through their website. When I searched Google just for *Palm and HP* I found articles on HP's acquisition of Palm—maybe these will provide some insight into their strategy. Some further digging is required, but you can see that you first have to step back and start broadly: Who is the parent company? What can you find on their website? What kind of reports can you find? What kind of articles can you find specifically about the Pixi or just in general about HP and marketing or HP and Palm and marketing? (Or even just about the smartphone industry and where the Pixi falls within it.)

There are lots of ways to approach this once you give yourself that distance and a little time to think. Share some of these ideas with the student and do probe like you did for clarification. Often students are starting with a specific product that they are familiar with and don't realize that they need to look at it within the larger context of the company that makes it (and that company name may not be the same as what they see on the product) as well as at the industry overall, so you can help to guide them through this research approach.

Q: My business reference stumper actually comes from a course assignment for an anthropology class on globalization. Students had to select a business of their choice and research the viability of setting up that business in a city in an emerging economy (for example, one student chose a restaurant in São Paulo, Brazil). Many types of information were required: demographic and socioeconomic information to determine whether there was an adequate labor supply and customer base, information on competitors in the area, tax policies, environmental and labor law, and licensing requirements, just to name a few. It is not that I was entirely stumped by the question, but the sheer amount of information required was a bit overwhelming, especially since this was during my first few weeks on the reference desk. I was able to find some information on these issues in sources I was familiar with, but my ability to rely on proper business information resources to help answer some of these questions was limited.

A: That is a tough kind of stumper where you not only have to find industry info, but country info, demographic info, and possibly international company info. I think your best approach to a multilayered question like this is to break it into chunks and remember not to try to drill down too granularly at first. In other words, you're setting yourself up for disappointment (usually) if you start with a search for the restaurant industry in São Paulo. It doesn't mean that you won't search for that kind of info eventually, but I'd start with some general searching on Brazil and São Paulo, on doing business in Brazil, on the restaurant industry in general, and go from there. Of course, try an article search and be as specific as you want, but also search broadly and look for clues along the way. Extrapolate from what you do find and encourage the students to make logical connections.

Also, this is the kind of question that has so many details that you may even want to check in with the professor and clarify what their expectations are. Often professors will assign something that they haven't really attempted to do themselves, and they may not realize the complexity involved in finding licensing requirements or tax policies, for example. You may find that they are fine with a broader approach and that they just want their students to show that they've thought some of these angles through, not necessarily to have exact data or regulations. This is helpful for you to know as you work with the students—you can help them through this thought process with that extra clarification from the professor. Oh, and since this was for an anthropology class on globalization, you could also look for general articles on topics like *globalization and restaurants and Brazil* (as one example) or maybe just *globalization and Brazil* or *globalization and restaurants* and find additional material to extrapolate from.

Again, don't get too caught up in the details in the beginning. See what you can find that is more general and how it might address some of the issues outlined in the assignment, and try to fill in the gaps.

STUMPERS: SMALL BUSINESS

Q: How would one go about exploring the process of selling a private corporation? This would include how to discover that it is for sale in the first place, how it gets advertised, and are there any legal filings that must occur to finalize a transaction? I am specifically interested in a company headquartered in Bohemia, New York. It is a private company and is partly owned by a private equity firm.

A: This is the kind of business stumper that calls also for legal expertise. I found a handy guide on selling your business on the Small Business Administration's website (www.sba.gov/smallbusinessplanner/exit/sellyourbusiness/). There looks to be some information on finding a buyer, sales agreements, and the like. Your local SBA might be also able to recommend lawyers who specialize in these kinds of transactions.

In this case, it sounds like there is also a private equity firm involved, so I'm thinking that they buy and sell businesses all the time. You might want to start looking around for information on how private equity firms operate to see if there are any clues as to what kinds of resources they use to find out what businesses are for sale, how and whom to sell them to, and so on. A quick search for *private equity associations and New York* shows that there are a few groups out there that you could perhaps contact to see if there was a local expert to walk you through the process. Also, it looks like several states have "business broker associations" that provide information about the selling of businesses, including (in the case of

Michigan, at least) a search engine for identifying businesses for sale. Just google *business broker association* and the state the patron is interested in.

It also looks like there are some books out there that provide some info on buying and selling businesses (you could ask your local SBA for recommendations).

Q: I am frequently asked about government loans and grants for starting a business. The publications with *free money* in the titles catch patrons' attention. Is there really free money?

A: I like to tell patrons that if there really were free money or a way to ride the next-big-thing wave, then I wouldn't be working in the library, now would I? That said, I think the short answer is "No . . . there's no free money." But for these kinds of questions, I'd point your patrons to some of the resources in chapter 10, "Small Business." The groups like the SBA and SCORE that are set up to support small businesses deal with these kinds of questions all the time and will know where to point people toward in terms of business grants, loans, etc. Don't forget to look at your local area business groups, such as chambers of commerce, as well as your municipal options (if you are near a big city, there will often be programs in place to help bring businesses in to build the tax base). Troll around the Internet to see what other kinds of small business guides you can find—maybe there is another library in your state that has a big entrepreneurial support program that you can "steal" from, or another library is doing something else that you could model.

Q: Every business question is a stumper for me. But recently, a patron who wants to start her own business—blacksmithing, horseshoeing—was searching for information on how to incorporate in Wyoming.

A: This sounds like a job for the local branch of the Wyoming Small Business Administration. Every state has its own local SBA (among other small business support entities). This has to be the kind of question that they answer all of the time. And since it is also likely to involve legal information, it's definitely best to refer rather than detail step by step (even if you've incorporated a business before and know what you're doing).

If the local SBA doesn't pan out, try to figure out which agency/organization in your local area is responsible for these kinds of administrative records. Companies have to register somewhere. It's possible your town hall or similar agency might have some info or know where to point you. But check on a local SBA first.

Q: One of the statistics we wanted to include in a grant proposal was the failure rate of small businesses in our region. We could find national statistics, but none of the agencies we contacted could give the local figure. Which, by the way, makes me wonder how the national figure is determined.

A: Here is another question where I would try to identify a source of the information before focusing on the answer itself. It sounds like in trying to answer the question you did come across some national numbers. I'd look at these to see where they were coming from and work up from there. If nothing else, you might be able to contact the source of the national-level numbers and find out if additional regional breakouts are available.

Also, I did a quick search for *failed businesses statistics* to see what kinds of clues I could find. One thing that came up was an old article from *Businessweek* that mentioned a number of studies by name (which you could then follow up on) as well as some of the specific areas of the census to get that kind of data. Also useful were mentions of some of the terminology, like *business starts and stops*. You could change around your search strategy to see if anything new or better came from that. I did also see in one article (www.businessweek.com/smallbiz/news/coladvice/ask/sa990930.htm) that the census only tracks closures of businesses that have employees—this may be a useful clue, too.

Finally, I'd check around with any other local/regional resources for small business (although it sounds like you're trying to start something up here). Who in the state is responsible for registering businesses? If you can identify them, you can maybe work back from there, as well.

Q: A patron asked what tax incentives and rebates the government offers businesses to encourage her to make physical improvements to make her business more "green."

A: This kind of question sounds like it has *small business* written all over it. I'd definitely check out some of the resources in chapter 10, "Small Business," and then also try to identify what kind of local area (city, county or state) small business resources there might be in your town. I wouldn't worry at first about specifically looking for green and tax incentives—if you can identify the small business resources first and then drill down, there may be sections that cover this and other tax incentives as well. It also wouldn't hurt to do a quick Google search for *tax incentives [your town/county/state] green or environment or energy* (or something similar) to see if anything is picked up or pointed to. There may also be some organizations that focus specifically on this topic. Don't forget—with any business reference question, it never hurts to ask "Who cares?" and see if it leads you to some resources.

And, speaking of who cares, in this case it doesn't hurt to ask around to anyone you know who is especially green. This question got me thinking about a former colleague who is now working with a group called Eco Achievers (http://ecoachievers.com). I did a quick check of their website and saw that it refers to a U.S. Green Building Council (www.usgbc.org). Lots of resources here, possibly with a focus on just homeowners, not small business owners, but you can probably get other terminology or keywords to try in additional searches.

STUMPERS: MISCELLANEOUS

Q: So I'm pretty new to business reference, and I find that I do well at showing students how to access and use the business resources that the school provides. But I often have trouble applying them to what they are learning because I have no business background. Other librarians at my institution experience the same thing. One librarian (not me, but it stumped me just the same) received a chat reference question that goes a little something like this: "What is the purpose of business research in preventing a loss in market share?"

Did the student take this question directly from a take-home test and think the librarian in the chat box would be able to answer it for him? Maybe. But nonetheless, it illustrated for us that we need to know more about business in general in order to help our students.

A: That's the first thing that I thought, too, when I saw that question—that the student was just trying to get you to do his (or her) homework. But just as you wouldn't answer a chat question like this: "How do Hamlet's seven soliloquies reveal his character?" neither would you just answer this one. Go back to the basics. Brush up the reference interview skills and don't be thrown by the fact that it's a *business* reference question. You can say, "It sounds like you're working on a class project. Is that true? Which class?" Don't forget to ask the student where he's already looked, and don't be afraid to ask for clarification: "Are you looking for a particular kind of market or business? What do you mean by business research?" In this case, I'm thinking that they're basically being asked to elaborate on why it's a good idea to know your industry, but pointing a student to a particular resource on this will be tricky. This may be an opportunity to also find out if it is a specific assignment and to maybe reach out to the faculty member who posed the question (if that is, in fact, the question that they're asking). You might be able to work with the faculty member to hone the assignment so that it's not only clearer for the students (and ties in better to whatever learning goals they are hoping to achieve and to the resources you have available) but clearer for you, as well.

Q: We have an assignment for a business ethics class where students have to find articles about some "ethical decision" made by an international/global company and it has to be fairly recent—within last few weeks. Any suggestions?

A: This is a tricky one, since overall it's quite subjective and open to interpretation. You may want to work with the students to pick a company or two to investigate specifically and then see if they can apply any of their recent actions to something related to ethics (Target's 2011 donation to a political group that backed a gubernatorial candidate who opposed gay rights and the backlash is something that comes to mind, but it would be hit or miss with whatever companies you were looking at).

Alternatively, I'd start to search around for business ethics news sites and resources . . . keeping in mind that there are different ways to describe business ethics, so that you could also be searching for *corporate social responsibility* or *governance* or possibly some other topics that might be seen by some as related to ethics (e.g., the environment, green supply chain, labor practices).

Don't be afraid to google at first and then use some of the clues that you find to help direct your search in an article database.

Q: My only business reference questions so far came from a faculty member who wanted articles on the effect of the economy on strategic decision making. How to search stumped me for a bit before I found some stuff.

A: This sounds similar in some ways to the previous question on global ethical decisions. It can be hard to find correlations between topics that aren't necessarily going to be described by the specific terminology. By that I mean, for example, that news about a company making an "ethical decision" probably won't be found with a search for *company and "ethical decision"*, so you have to come up with some creative ways to approach it. Same for this one. Of course, it never hurts to start with *economy and "strategic decision making"* and see what starts to come up, but you might want to narrow or broaden accordingly. Maybe just look at news articles on the economy and businesses in general and see if anything jumps out. You could look through some business school newsletters like *Working Knowledge* from Harvard to see what some of the discussions are. I think this is the kind of question that will take shape the more you dig around.

Don't forget, too, that when in doubt, it doesn't hurt to ask the patron some more questions. In this case, you might want to find out a little bit more about what the faculty member is working on. Are they looking for examples to use in a lecture? Are they working on an assignment for their students or an article themself? Just looking for some extra reading material? This can also help to guide your search and know better which results look the most promising.

Q: How to get grant money for a nonprofit organization?

A: We don't really cover nonprofit research very deeply in this book (it, like many of the other topics we do cover, could have a book all in itself), but there are definitely a lot of resources out there that focus on nonprofits. I'll point you to the page that I always find myself going to when faced with nonprofit-specific questions. It's a guide made by one of the subject specialists here at the U. of Michigan's main library: http://guides.lib.umich.edu/content.php?pid=22518. There are lots of other, similar guides out there that I would look for and maybe try to steal from to tailor to your own patron base.

Also, a quick search online on nonprofit funding (notice that I didn't limit it to just grants) pulls up quite a bit, including a USA.gov site devoted to the topic: www.usa.gov/Business/Nonprofit.shtml. You'll see that the first link on this list is to the Catalog of Federal Domestic Assistance (CDFA). As far as I know, this is considered kind of "the bible" of government grants. But there are likely many other grant resources and other funding sources as well.

Take a look through guides and then check locally to see if there are any groups in your area set up to help nonprofits specifically. It's also worth it to look through some of the resources discussed in chapter 10, "Small Business," to see if they cover nonprofits.

Q: Not sure if this is really a business reference stumper, but I was recently asked what a person needs to do if organizing a record show (where vinyl records are bought, traded, and sold by record enthusiasts). Are there permits necessary, or can a person just rent a space and do it?

A: This is a great question (and I, too, think it qualifies as business reference). I think you'd want to look into local venues where they might hold this kind of thing and ask about how groups set up shows, record-selling or otherwise. Also, if you have a local shop in town that still deals in vinyl (or music, at least), give them a call. They may well have experience in this (and maybe even offer to help out!). I know there was recently a "Record Store Day," so maybe for information specific to record sales, they might have some answers, too: www.recordstoreday.com.

Really, though, I would guess that this would be akin to holding a flea market or something like that, so figuring out where and how those get organized would likely do the trick. There will probably be some local restrictions/permits/quirks, so it's probably best to identify a venue first and see what they can tell you.

Q: Is spin welding still the most economical way to join and fasten plastics? If not, what's better? Under what circumstances should spin welding not be used? Is there grant money available for plastics fusion technology, or has the industry gone completely over to injection molding?

A: Hmmm . . . this sounds like multiple stumpers! I'd start with a search for information (probably online and with some article searching) on *plastic fastening/*

fusion and spin welding and injection molding. Look around for associations and other groups that might have this kind of info (and be aware that the Spin Welding Association may well say that their way is still the best way, while the Other Plastic Fastening Method X Association says their way is the best). Don't forget to step back and look for general info on engineering processes and plastics, too, and be on the lookout for clues.

As for grant money, I'd look through some of the resources in chapter 10, "Small Business," and any other funding resources you may have (local or regional) to see if anything aligns with plastics in general. Also identify whether there are any related programs at nearby universities to see what they may have going on.

Q: This question is part of a much bigger reference question for a patron who was looking to change careers. Although I found a lot of information about jobs in the financial industry, I was never able to locate a complete answer to the following questions: "What is the salary range for financial salespeople (various positions) at specific companies (e.g., Merrill Lynch) in specific metropolitan areas (e.g., Denver)? Also, what percentage of annual compensation comes from commission (versus base salary pay) in these positions?"

I was able to locate general information on salaries from the American Salaries and Wages Survey, but the information was not specific enough for the patron. Websites like Salary.com also seemed to provide information that was too general. I tried databases like Mergent, but the positions that listed salary for specific companies were all at higher position levels.

Any ideas?

A: This kind of question falls into the "proprietary company info" category, and from the sounds of it you've done all you can do to get what you can. Finding specific salaries for specific companies in specific locations is just getting down to a granular level that won't happen. And, in this case, the question is even harder because the patron wants to have the salary broken down into commission versus base salary—sheesh! You were smart to go to general salary reference sources and then to try some online sites. My only other suggestion would be to go to some job sites, maybe specifically financial ones like Vault (www.vault.com) and WetFeet (www.wetfeet.com), and do some searching to see if there are any ranges given (even in specific job announcements, though they rarely list actual salaries, plus you have to keep in mind the other nonsalary benefits such as health care, stock options, bonuses, etc.). And the reason Mergent and other business databases may have some salary info on the higher-up positions is because companies are required to disclose this info to the SEC.

One other suggestion that just came to mind is that you could also try to identify a trade association for financial professionals and see if anyone there can point to a mentor or to someone in the industry who might be able to talk to the patron. Similarly, maybe there's a college nearby with a finance program and a student group that offers career assistance. If they can find someone who does what they're looking to do, they might get some of this salary information as well as additional networking ideas. Just a long-shot idea, though.

Q: A patron wanted the formula for determining menu prices for a restaurant. My branch did not have any books on running a restaurant. I showed her our online Gale business plans handbook and suggested that she review all the restaurant business plans (there were six). Next, I suggested searching in the Business and Company Resource Center. I also suggested checking with UCF's College of Hospitality library. She was happy to leave with something to try (it was closing time).

A: That is *such* a five-minutes-before-closing question! And you did exactly the right thing. That's not the kind of thing you're just going to find with a quick Google search. Looking at business plans for restaurants and other industry sources is the best place to start, and referring her to a hospitality library is genius! Business and Company Resource Center might have had something on restaurants, but that might be a better source for looking up some basic industry info than specific data on pricing formulas. I might have also shown her a business-article database and given her some tips for searching for menus and pricing, but it sounds like she got a great start and can follow up with a specialty library to boot.

Q: Since I am so new, I have not actually had any stumpers yet. So I queried my ref colleagues and they all agree that this is an all-time favorite: "What is the percentage of soft drinks in plastic bottles and aluminum cans compared to the percentage of beer in plastic bottles and aluminum cans?"

Apparently it took a team several hours to figure this one out!

A: You mean you don't know the answer to this off the top of your head? Or have you never heard of "the encyclopedia of soft drinks and beer and the containers they love"?

I'm hoping that by now you've seen some tips from chapter 4, "Industry Research," to give you some ideas for how to approach this kind of question. Looking at some of the industry reports related to alcohol or beverages in general, or aluminum can manufacturing or bottling, might provide some clues. In this case, I'd try to identify industry associations for can and bottle manufacturers and then do the ol' literature search looking for articles on *beer and soft drinks and containers* (and all the other synonyms you can think of). You'll either hit the jackpot or at least be pointed to some good sources of info that you can follow up on. But I'm not surprised that it took a team of people a while to get this. Sounds like they're still recovering!

Q: I took a poll here, and we all agreed that the most frustrating question we get every semester is for the assignment where the students must find industry regulations. Is there a standard place to look for that?

A: Don't worry—as far as I know, you're not missing any "standard" resources for finding industry regulations. As you can see from chapter 4, "Industry Research," there's a lot that goes into just finding basic industry info, let alone a comprehensive source for regulations. It will also depend on the industry in question. I did a quick Google search for *industry regulations site:.edu library* (to see if any academic libraries pointed to some resources) and found a handy flowchart from UCLA that addresses competitive intelligence research: www.anderson.ucla.edu/x14441 .xml#C-1. There is a section on looking into regulations that will affect your company, and it lists a few resources, like the Federal Regulatory Directory and the Code of Federal Regulations.

With any kind of legal question like this (especially if it is part of a recurring assignment), I'd dig a little and find out just how in-depth an answer is being looked for. Is this for a basic business class? Or for a third-year law class? You may want to talk to the professor and find out their expectations. As I mentioned in another stumper, often professors haven't ever actually done the assignment themselves and are surprised to find that what they're asking for isn't readily available. Or you may find that the students are misinterpreting an assignment one way or another.

Q: Trick index question: A patron came up to the desk and wanted to see "the oil index, the gold index, and the food index." I completely agree about not knowing the language of business and wanting to become more comfortable with it. Recently I read *Law for Dummies* and took a workshop on some legal databases we offered taught by our legal specialist. The result? I realized that even though the patron might be using jargon and projecting an air of confidence, he might not really know what he's talking about and is, in fact, asking you for something that doesn't even exist!

A: Yes, you'll often find that some patrons don't like to admit that they really don't know what they are talking about—just repeating terms used by a professor or colleague or heard on the street. A good reference interview to clarify the "real" question is a must. With any subject area, really, you have to watch out for "fakers," but for some reason business (and law, too, for sure) brings them out of the woodwork. Frankly, even if someone *does* know what they're talking about, it's not helping anyone to just throw around lingo and expect everyone to understand.

It's like yelling loudly when someone doesn't speak the same language . . . hearing is not the issue! Flex those reference interview (and people skills) muscles and try to find out what they're *really* trying to do—and don't let anyone fool you or intimidate you.

Q: We had a student who was looking for a company that has been though a lot of changes in the past five years. It was handed off to someone with more experience, but I always wonder where they went and what changes he was talking about.

A: This sounds intriguing. I wonder if the student was merely supposed to come up with an example company and then do a little research and document the changes. As far as I know, there isn't a particular resource that is going to only track company "changes." And, of course, "changes" can mean a lot of things. You'd want to talk more with the patron and find out what would qualify. A new CEO? A big marketing campaign? An SEC investigation? You'd look up each of these topics in different places, most likely. This would be the kind of question you'd want to do a little thinking about before diving into a search, since searching for *company and change* isn't going to be too helpful, probably. In the end, if you were still hitting a wall, I'd follow up with the professor to get her input on the assignment. It may be more straightforward than it seems.

Q: I have a basic knowledge of the online census and American FactFinder. Whenever I use data sets and actually find an answer I feel like I stumbled upon it by pure luck. I'm never sure if I've looked through the right sections (or all the sections) that I should have.

A: Well, I'm afraid my advice here is practice, practice, practice. I know what you mean, though, about feeling like you've only stumbled across the right answer because the planets are in alignment that day and you happened to catch American FactFinder in a good mood. Hopefully some of the tips in chapters 4, "Industry Research," and 8, "Business (and Other) Statistics," will give you some ideas for maximizing your searching within the census and with FactFinder. These are two tools that could have their own classes themselves . . . and it's possible they do—look into local library groups/conferences and see if you can find an expert or workshop. Alternatively, if you find that you're starting to be really good at navigating the ins and outs of the census, share your knowledge with colleagues and offer an in-service training (in other words, be careful for wishing to get good at this). And, if you find that you get lots of the same kinds of questions, write down how you got to the right data and make it that much easier the next time it comes up, for you or for someone else. Finally, look around to see if there are local groups that have made some of your more common searches easier. For example, in Chicago there is something called the Metro Chicago Information Center. They've built their own interface that uses census data but that drills down to Chicago-specific areas—much easier to use theirs than to try to do the same thing with American FactFinder.

One last word on American FactFinder: any tool that provides *so much* data is going to come with a cost, whether that's in monetary value or in the time it takes you to be proficient in using the system, or both. So don't think it's any shortcoming on your part that you're not swooshing down that triple diamond slope just seconds after getting off the bunny trail. While it would be great to have everything be one or two clicks away, when we're getting deep into statistics and other hairy topics, it's just not as simple as that (at least not most of the time, unfortunately).

Q: Where can you find detailed biographies of CEOs and other company leaders?

A: The answer to this one is "it depends." While there is a reference source called the International Directory of Business Biographies, by no means are you going to find everyone in there.

Speaking of the International Directory of Business Biographies: I wrote the entry for Staples CEO Ron Sargent. I can tell you from writing it that I had to sift through many resources, mostly articles, to compile it. I even tried to call the company and his personal assistant to try to confirm details, but I never heard back. There is a bibliography at the end which will help to illustrate all of the different resources that went into compiling the entry. Here's a link to a free online version of the entry: www.referenceforbusiness.com/biography/S-Z/Sargent-Ron-1955.html.

The International Directory of Business Biographies is a Gale Cengage Learning product, and the content may be included in their Business and Company Resource Center product or their new Business Insights: Global. Here's a link to the Gale description: http://gale.cengage.com/servlet/ItemDetailServlet?region=9&imprint=000&titleCode=&type=2&id=194442.

For whatever reason, many CEOs and other company leaders try to keep their biographical info fairly private, some companies more so than others (e.g., Trader Joe's is notorious for their secrecy). There is some directory-type info in NetAdvantage—you can find out where various CEOs went to college. Bloomberg (the full subscription) offers a similar brief bio for many corporate leaders. For the most part, though, you'll have to sift through articles. If you know where they are from, you can look for hometown newspapers which may have done features. Many trade journals also profile corporate leaders. You may want to add terms such as *biography* or *profile* to your search to avoid pulling up hundreds of articles that just mention the name. Also, with name searching, be wary of first name–last name order, middle initials, and nicknames. Put in clues sparingly—maybe a fairly unusual last name and a company name (or two) that you know they are associated with.

But even for lesser-known individuals this kind of searching may be difficult. You may have to go with whatever you can find on the company website.

Q: How do you evaluate the "greenness" or social responsibility factor of various mutual funds? Is there a trustworthy outside organization that judges or ranks them? Is there a compilation of such funds that can be looked at for comparison?

A: Corporate social responsibility (CSR) is a big area now, although, like many business reference areas, there are not really any hard and fast ways that you can evaluate a company through this lens. However, there are a growing number of resources in this area. A great resource/primer in this area, if I do say so myself, is the "Clean, Green and Not So Mean: Can Business Save the World" article that was a result of the BRASS Chair's program last year in Washington, DC (when I was, ahem, BRASS chair). Here's a link to the article/conference summary: www.rusq.org/2010/12/29/clean-green-and-not-so-mean-can-business-save-the-world/. It points to some great resources in this area. It also discusses the nature of trustworthiness in terms of evaluation.

Also, this is another area where looking for a guide can be useful. I did a quick Google search for *csr library site:.edu* and was pointed to this guide from Cornell: http://guides.library.cornell.edu/content.php?pid=77511&sid=580907. Click on the tabs and you'll see references to databases like Innovest and Socrates. These are useful tools for evaluating funds and stocks.

Some databases are also starting to incorporate CSR tools into their products. For example, Morningstar Investment Research Center has a guide to green/socially responsible investing. They also have a screen in their Funds tab.

You can also always fall back on the tried-and-true strategy of an article search—look for articles on your company and terms like *green* or *environmental* or *sustainability* or *csr*, etc., and see what comes up. And a few other resources are pointed to in chapter 6, "Investment Research."

Q: I have a background in English lit, so finding good language to construct effective searches for business questions is always a challenge for me. One I recently had a lot of trouble with (although I'm sure there's all kinds of published info out there) was the following: "I need peer-reviewed articles about the advantages and disadvantages of using consulting firms to examine/redesign internal corporate organizational structures."

At least, I think that's what the student was asking. We had some success, but nothing really meaty or in depth.

A: With this kind of stumper, as with many others, I'd try to step back and parse it out, so to speak. I see a couple of concepts here, one being the effectiveness of consulting firms, another being redesigning organizational structures.

I'd worry about whether what you're finding is peer-reviewed after you've, in fact, found something. I don't usually limit my searching to peer-reviewed only at first simply because you may miss out on a useful article or other resource. Some people, faculty members included, are surprised to find that the *Harvard Business Review* and similarly respected journals are not considered "scholarly" (because they're not peer-reviewed), and it might actually be okay to use something like that. And even if you don't end up using it as one of your final sources, it still might point you through clues in the text to something else that is scholarly/peer-reviewed.

As I've mentioned before, don't be afraid to encourage your patrons to make some logical leaps. Maybe you can find some good articles on best practices related to organizational restructuring and some articles on best practices in using consulting firm services and extrapolate from there. Don't get tunnel vision and only focus on looking for exactly the answer to the question. It's really easy to get bogged down with the various terms thrown around in questions like these, but remember that less is more when it comes to searching—stick to the broader language at first and don't worry about terms such as, in this case, *internal corporate organizational structures*. If you're searching using those terms, you'll be far too limited. *Internal* and *corporate* are sort of beside the point. Focus on the broader concept of *organizational structures* or terms such as *reorganization or restructuring* (and maybe you'll find that some of these terms show up in an article as you search) and the broader concepts of *consulting* or *consultants* and go from there. There will be a lot of back-and-forth and honing of your search, but that's normal (and, if you think about it, it's what you'd do in a non-business-topic kind of search, too, except that it's easy to forget this for some reason when the subject matter is business).

INDEX

Page numbers in bold indicate topics covered in the Stumpers Q&A section.